D1259622

The Lost Art of Economics

The Lost Art of Economics: Essays on Economics and the Economics Profession

David Colander
Christian A. Johnson Distinguished Professor of Economics,
Middlebury College, Vermont, USA

Edward Elgar
Cheltenham, UK · Northampton, MA, USA

Published by
Edward Elgar Publishing Limited
Glensanda House
Montpellier Parade
Cheltenham
Glos GL50 1UA
UK

Edward Elgar Publishing, Inc.
136 West Street
Suite 202
Northampton
Massachusetts 01060
USA

A catalogue record for this book
is available from the British Library

Library of Congress Cataloguing in Publication Data

Colander, David C.
    The lost art of economics : economics and the economics profession / David
Colander.
        p. cm.
    Includes bibliographical references and index.
    1. Economics–Study and teaching–History. 2. Economists. 3. Economics–
Vocational guidance. I. Title.

    HB74.5 .C654 2001
    330'.09–dc21

                                                                2001023353

ISBN 1 84064 694 2

Printed and bound in Great Britain by Bookcraft (Bath) Ltd.

Contents

PART VI: THE FUTURE OF THE ECONOMICS PROFESSION

Preface

As my views about economics and the economy have become better known, I've had a number of invitations to write or speak on the economics profession. A collection of those essays came out in *Why Aren't Economists as Important as Garbagemen* (Sharpe, 1990), which I'm happy to say was well received. This book is a continuation of the ideas in that volume. It shows the evolution of my thinking about the profession, my views of what has occurred, and what I think will occur in the future.

The chapters are self-contained essays so they can be read selectively. Moreover, they are written in a style accessible to all interested scholars, although there are some aspects of the book that economists will understand better than non-economists will. To make the book more readable by everyone, in the introduction I have provided background material about the academic subsection of the economics profession, summarized the central arguments in my *Garbagemen* book to put the current essays in perspective, and provided an overview of the arguments in the essays.

The essays in this book are meant to be a fun read. There is too much in economics that is so deep that the reader doesn't know what is being said. It might be important, but it is hard to figure out how or why. I favor straight, to-the-point writing that glosses over some of the esoteric issues, and focuses on the central issues relevant to a broad audience. Thus, the essays tell a simple story—one of economists focusing a bit too much on models, and not quite enough on educated common sense. They are written not so much to criticize economists as to awaken their workmanship instinct, and to encourage them to change.

Acknowledgments

All books involve an enormous amount of work by many more people than the author, and this one is no different. I would like to thank a number of people who made this book poosible. This includes my wife and kids, who let this one slip by even though I promised not to do another book this year; my students, who keep putting new ideas into my head; Melissa Dasakis, for assistance in editing; Helen Reiff, who proofread much of the book, helped get the manuscript in shape, and did the index; Pam Bodenhorn, who typeset the book and helped proof it; Jenifer Gamber, who helped in composition work; Dave Horlacher, Paul Streeten, and Tom Mayer who in reading the page proofs caught important errors; and Sonia Ignatoua, who did important bibliographic work on the book. And finally, there are the people at Edward Elgar – Edward, who when he saw me at the AEA meetings, put the idea into my head, jotted it down in his little notebook, and followed up on it by sending me a contract and asking me when I was getting to that book I promised him (without his methodical prodding, this book would never be) – and his staff: Julie Leppard, Matt Pittman, Bob Pickens, and Christine Gowen.

Variations of these essays were published in a variety of places, and I would like to thank the American Economic Association, Taylor and Francis Publishers, Routledge Publishers, the University of Michigan Press, Heldref Publishers, Blackwell Publishers, Sharpe Publishers, and Edward Elgar Publishers for giving me permission to reprint them. The places where the previously appeared are the following:

- "The Lost Art of Economics," *Journal of Economic Perspectives*, Summer, 1992.
- "Is Milton Friedman an Artist or a Scientist?" *Journal of Economic Methodology*, 1995.
- "The Art of Economics by the Numbers" in *Recent Developments in Methodology*, Roger Backhouse, ed., 1994.
- "The Art of Monetary Policy" (with Dewey Daane) in *The Art of Monetary Policy* (David Colander andDewey Daane, eds): Sharpe 1994.
- "Telling Better Stories in Introductory Macro," *American Economic Review*, May 2000.
- "Teaching Keynes in the 21st Century," *Journal of Economic Education*, 30 (4), Fall 1999.

- "Confessions of an Economic Gadfly," *Passion and Craft: Economists at Work* (Michael Szensberg, ed.): University of Michigan Press, 1998.
- "Surviving as a Slightly Out of Sync Economist," in *A Guide to How to Do Economics* (Steven Medema and Warren Samuels, eds.): Edward Elgar, 1996.
- "The Sounds of Silence: The Profession's Response to the *COGEE Report*," *Journal of Agricultural Economics*, 1998.
- "Vision, Judgment, and Disagreement among Economists," *Journal of Economic Methodology,* 1994.
- "The Death of Neoclassical Economics," *Journal of the History of Economic Thought*, June 2000.
- "New Millennium Economics: How Did it Get This Way, and What Way is It?" *Journal of Economic Perspectives*, 14 (1), Winter 1999.

Introduction

I'm an economist watcher; it's not as much fun as being a girl watcher, but it's fun nonetheless. By watching economists you see how reasonably normal people, through seven or so years of intensive graduate training, are transformed into the model-driven, number-crunching individuals who are recognizable everywhere as economists. Actually there is no formal "union card" required of economists; anyone is free to call him or herself an economist. There is, however, an informal union card and it's a tough one to get. To be considered an "economist" by another union-card economist one needs a Ph.D. in economics, and it is this subgroup of economists that I watch, focusing on academic economists.

Within this set of union-card economists there are also rankings. Conversations with newly-met economists often begin with "Where did you get your Ph.D.?" Upon hearing where, the questioner will make a judgment about the quality of one's training and whether or not one should be considered a serious economist. (It's a bit like two dogs marking out their territory.) If you are planning to go on in serious economic research, you had better be able to answer that question with "I went to (fill in the name of one of the twenty of the top-ten-ranked economics graduate programs)."[1] Otherwise you don't pass the initial sniff test.

Once one becomes a card-carrying economist there are a variety of jobs one can get—in business, in government, and in academia. Of these, academia is the most highly ranked; the needs and desires of academics drive the profession.

THE STRUCTURE OF THE PROFESSION

The composition of the economics profession is in large part male, and to a considerable degree foreign. The top ten programs are dominated by foreign students; according to published accounts they make up more than 50 percent of the student body in graduate schools (Aslanbeigui and Montecinos, 1998). My count of the number of foreign students at top schools is even higher. At two schools that I looked at almost the entire incoming class were foreign students. Why the difference? I suspect it is because foreign students are less likely to fill out questionnaires, and because there are a few programs,

1

such as Berkeley's, where there are mostly American students. (Why Berkeley? It's because of California's requirement that scholarships at state schools such as Berkeley cannot be given to foreign students.)

The existence of so many foreign economists is due to a number of factors. First, US graduate schools are considered the best worldwide, so the market for Ph.D. students must be considered global. In a global market we would not expect most students to be from the United States. Second, graduate school in economics is not an attractive option for many bright US students. It requires a stronger background in math and statistics than most have, and those who do have the background have a variety of opportunities that offer more rewards sooner. Choosing six years of the relative poverty and deprivation of a graduate student's life over an investment banking job where the starting salary is anywhere from $75,000 to $100,000 a year and the expectations are of earning in the millions in six years is a choice only the highly-committed or the uninformed will make. Thus, I am not surprised that all my top US students, and most of my top foreign students, have not chosen economics programs.

The foreign students going on in top-ten economics programs are top students. Their English is generally impeccable, and they are extraordinarily well trained and bright. Those who have been to undergraduate school in the United States were at the top of their classes there. Those who haven't often have advanced degrees in mathematics or statistics. They are in graduate economics because they are good and are committed to economics, not because they don't have other options.

At lower-ranked schools, the story is more mixed; besides the top students with not-so-good information about the ranking of US programs, at these schools there are a number of foreign students who are using economics graduate school as a method of immigrating to the United States.

Graduate economics programs are also predominantly male. About two-thirds of all graduate economics students in top-ten programs are men and about three-quarters of the students in top-ten programs are men. The higher up you go, the fewer women you find.[2] The percentage of women in tenure track positions at top schools is about 6 percent. The scarcity of women is generally attributed to the mathematics in the program and the generally inhospitable nature economics training programs extend to women. There is a small feminist movement in economics, but it is heterodox—outside the academic mainstream of economics.

AFTER GRADUATION: THE BARRACUDA POOLS

Less than 70 percent of those who start top graduate economics programs finish; the others get an M.A., go off to some other program, or get a job that doesn't require a Ph.D. in economics. For those who do graduate, there is an enormous pressure to take an academic research job as an assistant professor, ideally at one of the top ten schools. I call assistant professor jobs the barracuda pool because they are cutthroat and because the jobs drive their holders to make a splash. Less than 50 percent of those will get tenure at their first job; the others will be eaten alive by the publish-or-perish system that rules the first seven years of one's academic life.

Professors who don't make tenure in their initial pools have a number of options; some proceed to a lower ranked school, some proceed to teaching positions at undergraduate colleges, and some move on to business, government, or international agency research positions. A few may even decide to head off and take that investment banking position they turned down when they entered graduate school, although they have a strike against them because, simply by going to graduate school, they have already demonstrated that they are too cerebral to be real investment bankers.

As I hope I have made clear, the survivors of the top ten barracuda pools are only a small percentage of the profession. They, however, are the elite. They will be the stars; they form the cutting edge, and the direction that their work takes will determine the direction of the profession.

Once one gets tenure, one can slow down, and many of them do. But others keep on working intensely because of social pressures at their school, because of an inner drive, and because their love of doing economics has not been killed off by the grueling years in the barracuda pool. A few turn away from technical research toward more general public research, writing textbooks and popular articles and books. Once one is tenured at a top-ten school, it is much easier to have a voice and be published in that broader public policy arena.

The elite are, by definition, only a small percentage of the profession. The majority of those going on into academia find themselves in the little barracuda pool, the pool of assistant professor positions at the hundred schools in the top forty schools in the ranking.[3] In this pool you churn out "research" in much the same way that you do at the top schools, but the expectations are slightly different depending on whether your department is on the make—trying to move up in the rankings—or has given up that dream. At an "on the make" school, tenure requirements can often be more demanding than those at an actual top-ten school. A friend of mine was dean at an "on the make" school. One year six economists came up for tenure and one was offered it; he left for an offer at another school. When asked about this record my friend said, "I guess we chose the right one."

At lower-ranked schools, quantitative publication requirements are often more specific. Getting tenure at lower-ranked schools can mean publishing more articles than at the top schools. The difference is that they do not have to be the "quality" articles that change the direction of research or otherwise make a big splash in the profession.

At some small barracuda pools, especially those that are unionized, the tenure requirements are even translated into a number. Journals are given weights that are determined by one of the many publicly available rankings of the journal (a ReStat article might be worth .64 of an equal-length JPE article), by the length of the article (adjusted for size of page and type), by whether the article was co-authored (usually half credit for one co-author), and a variety of other criteria. Then there are all the modifications that must be made to these. (A publication in the May AER is different than a publication in the June AER.) I've seen specifications of these modifications go for 25 pages or more! At such schools research is a quantifiable commodity.

The schools that have given up any dream of making it in the top ten fall into the "contented" or "sleeper" categories. The contented have chosen a specialty that their school focuses on. They hire primarily in that area and they train their students primarily in that area. They do what they do, and they do it well. They don't aim for the same set of journals and they have their own criteria for success. The sleepers are programs where the majority of professors aren't trying to excel in any research area; the professors at these schools are happy in their tenure and they do their job. They teach and they publish occasionally. At these schools there is not the pressure on assistant professors to publish and succeed as there is at other schools. Professors at a sleeper school are probably the most well-rounded of all professors. They are content with their families, their consulting, or their academic politics at their school, each of which can become a full-time job on its own.

ALTERNATIVES TO THE BARRACUDA POOL

Professors who don't make tenure in these pools have options similar to those who didn't make tenure at a top-ten school. Like their counterparts some proceed to a lower-ranked school, some can proceed to teach at an undergraduate college, some move on to private agency research positions, and others move on to business, government, or international agency research positions. These are all highly-respected positions.

These non-graduate school academic jobs are not consolation prizes for all economists. Not everyone aspires to graduate school life. A number of incoming graduate students plan right from the start to go into undergraduate teaching jobs or policy jobs. However, students entering graduate school with such plans face constant pressure in graduate school to change their goals. And if they let their teaching or policy ambitions be known they will likely be treated as second-class citizens. But if a student is willing to put up with being a second-class citizen throughout graduate school, and can withstand the social pressures to adopt the graduate school academic research mentality, there is a whole different ranking system that is more open. For these students the graduate program in economics is a hoop they must jump through to reach what they want to do. This group is the group I hang around with; it has, however, very little influence in the profession; you won't see its members on the executive committee of the AEA or in one of the AEA offices.

MY HISTORY AS AN ECONOMIST WATCHER

Being an economist watcher is a bit incestuous since I'm an academic economist myself. I somehow made it through the graduate school experience relatively unscathed. I suspect the reason is my hardheadedness. I also remained outside of the graduate school barracuda pool; I went on to teach at top undergraduate schools, which gives me a nice perch to watch from. I'm close enough to walk and talk with the "real economists," but far enough away to maintain some perspective.

I wrote my first economist-watching book, *Why Aren't Economists as Important as Garbagemen,* about ten years ago. It contained a selection of essays about the training of economists, their activities, and their foibles. This book is a continuation of that book, so let me review the central ideas in the *Garbagemen* book.

The overriding idea in the *Garbagemen* book was a simple one; it was that economists had made themselves far less relevant than they could be because they focused on deductive models that led to publications, but that were not especially useful in developing relevant insights about policy. In playing the academic game, economists often lost sight of the simple fact that economics was primarily about policy, not logical games. It recounted the study (1987, 1990) Arjo Klamer and I did of top graduate economics programs that showed that a knowledge of institutions and literature has become less important to economists' thinking.

Specifically, we asked students what will likely place students on the fast track within the economics profession. Knowledge of the economy and knowledge of economic literature did not make an economist successful, according to graduate students. Forty-three percent believed that a knowledge of economic literature was unimportant, while only 10 percent felt that it was very important. Sixty-eight percent believed that a thorough knowledge of the economy was unimportant; only 3 percent believed it was very important.

What did graduate students believe was important for succeeding as an economist? Modeling. Sixty-five percent said that being smart in the sense of being good at problem solving was very important and 57 percent said that excellence in mathematics was very important. Only 3 and 2 percent respectively felt that these qualities were unimportant.

Our conclusion from that study was that economists were often losing sight of the ultimate purpose of doing the modeling: to provide insight into policy issues. Educated common sense was replaced with formal structure, either mathematically or statistically.

In explaining how this state of affairs came about, I turned economic analysis upon itself, and considered economists as utility maximizers operating within an academic institutional structure. I argued that the problems in the economics profession could be predicted by economic theory. In economists' jargon academic institutions had severe incentive compatibility problems. Economists focused on models because it was in their institutional interest to do so. The problem, I argued, was not one of economists; it was a problem of institutional structure. The incentives in academic institutions were skewed and were not being properly translated into what I believed to be the correct social goals.

To me, the correct social goal is for economists to provide as much insight into policy issues, and to understanding the economy, as possible. The majority of academic institutions translated that ultimate goal into quantifiable intermediate goals—publications in the right journals and winning the latest academic debate—with little concern about how relevant those intermediate goals were for the real world. Economists' individual incentives were to publish in those sets of journals that lead to tenure, promotion, and internal fame.

A set of publication criteria developed in each journal that became more and more removed from the ultimate goal. Too few economists asked: Is this paper furthering our understanding of the economy? Instead they judged the paper on its use of models and its technical prowess in statistical testing of "the model." In Deirdre McCloskey's terminology, they never asked "how big?"

The economics profession is not unique; many professions and businesses have similar problems in translating social goals into measurable individual incentives that direct individuals to work for the greater social goal. Thus, the argument I made in the *Garbagemen* book was not that economics was unique, but simply that it had problems and the time had come to deal with those problems and restructure the institutional incentives.

I argued that the push for restructuring had to come from the workmanship instinct of the members of the profession because the economics profession is only indirectly subject to market pressures. When for-profit businesses have incentive problems, they lose profits and market share, and the market thereby encourages them to change. We've seen a lot of businesses making that change over the last decade in the United States. But economics is part of academia;

it is not a for-profit business, and hence does not face the same market pressures. In a non-market setting such as academia, the pressure for change must come from within.

ASKING TOO MUCH FROM ECONOMISTS

In that book I also explored why the incentives had become skewed. I argued that it was because economists had set up an impossible task for themselves—and that they had a fundamentally incorrect view of the nature of their role in society. They were trained to view themselves as outside observers of the economy—looking down on the economy from above. From that outside perspective they were to make judgments on how well the economy was functioning.

But placing economists outside the process left the problem of who would judge the judges, a concern that economists took to heart. In trying to ensure that their research was value-free, they developed a welfare economics guide for policy based upon Pareto Optimality that essentially eliminated their having a direct role in policy. In the quest for ideological purity they developed a formal analysis that eliminated their policy role.

THEORETICAL APPLIED POLICY AND ACTUAL APPLIED POLICY

Society needs economists in policy roles, and continually turns to them when it has policy questions concerning economics, even though economists' training does not prepare them to work in policy roles. In a sense, I argued, there was a first-floor policy economics to supplement the third-floor theoretical economics, using the metaphor Edward Leamer (1983) used in his article on how econometrics was theoretically taught and how it was actually done. One learns one set of theoretical approaches to policy problems on the third floor and a second set of practical approaches to problems on the first floor. What was done on the first floor would be considered sinning on the third floor, but is necessary sinning if one is going to arrive at policy conclusions.

Basing their analysis on what they learned on the first floor, economists have provided an active policy role. They devise models whose express purpose is to arrive at policy results. At the end of just about every academic article, one will see a small policy section explaining the implications of the model for policy.

Despite appearance to the contrary, this focus on policy does not contradict

the argument I made above that we cannot draw policy conclusions from theoretical economic models. If you force individuals to do something, they will
do it, even if it is impossible. But doing the impossible often requires some
sleight of hand, and not too careful scrutiny of its true implications. Most
economists' applied policy analysis based on abstract models does not stand
up to careful scrutiny. As opposed to saying, "I am premising this policy argument on these value judgments," they argued as if the policy followed from
economic theory. So we had the worst of both worlds.

A few, highly theoretical, economists stayed true to formal theory and general equilibrium, and found that their analysis provided little in the way of
usable policy advice. Examples include Robert Lucas (Klamer, 1984, p.54)
who, when asked what he would do if he were appointed to the Council of
Economic Advisors, said, "Resign," and Gerard Debreu who, when asked
about the relevance of his work to economic policy, said it had none.

The majority of economists did not follow this path; they gave up formal
theory and approached policy using a number of *ad hoc* models that fit the
data but was did not maintain full consistency with general equilibrium assumptions. If rationality didn't seem to fit, they chose to use a model not
based on rationality, but instead on some psychological regularity. This, of
course, left the work open to charges of *ad hoc*ness, and it has often been
attacked on that basis, but applicability was preferred to irrelevance.

The empirical work that economists did was attacked on many fronts. It
was pointed out that the models do not neatly fit the reality, and that the
researchers generally massaged the data and used proxies for variables. All
economists knew this is what was done. Cooley and Thomas have described
the result as a "zero-communication informational equilibrium," in which
"the researcher has the motive and opportunity to present his results selectively, and the reader, knowing this, imputes a low or zero signal-to-noise
ratio to the reported results" (Cooley and Leroy, 1981, p. 826). Faced with
these attacks, these applied economists were even more careful to make the
presentation look impressive and forbidding.

In the *Garbagemen* book, I did not fault applied economists for making
these *ad hoc* assumptions, nor for doing dirty empirical work. I believe it is
absolutely necessary if one is going to do reasonable applied policy work. I
faulted them only for making the work look more scientific than it actually is,
and it actually could be.[4]

In the *Garbagemen* book I also suggested a solution; I argued that the
appropriate role for economists was a less demanding one. Instead of viewing
themselves as outside observers of the economy, they should see themselves
as inside observers. Their existence reflected society's investment in protect-
ing, modifying, and changing economic institutions. Since anyone inside
had to have values, and had to be tainted, economists no longer had to strive

for the impossible—to attain ideological purity. For conservatives, this meant giving up the presumption that economic theory led to the conclusion that the market was the best approach. For liberals it meant modifying their form of argumentation. The economic theory of the market they use cannot lead one to a policy position that the government should or should not intervene independent of the political judgments.

The *Garbagemen* book went over quite well, although probably for the wrong reasons. People like economist-bashing books, especially if they're written by another economist (it's a bit like their attraction to dog fights). But my book wasn't really about bashing economists. It was more about bringing into the open some problems the profession had, and knew about, but preferred not to talk about. It was airing dirty laundry. Now every profession has dirty laundry, but most are quite hesitant to air it out in public. I find such airing cathartic; it forces the profession to face up to problems that it otherwise would avoid.

RECENT CHANGES IN THE PROFESSION

The profession has changed since I wrote that book. Economics in 2000 is not economics in 1990. It changed, not because of the arguments in my book, but because my understanding of the profession was not unique; I simply put it into words. The profession has a strong instinct for workmanship, and that feeling was pushing the research and work to more policy relevance, and to take better care when doing policy models. Ironically, in doing so, it has become more, not less, mathematical.

I see movement towards greater mathematical sophistication as a positive step. My problem with economics has never been the use of mathematics; my problem has always been the use of what I considered inappropriate mathematics. With developments in non-linear dynamics and recursive function theory, combined with the growth in computational technology and agent-based modeling, the applicability of mathematics to economics is expanding.

My current belief is that in the upcoming decades gains in complexity science are likely to revolutionize the way economics is done, with an enormous increase in simulation and agent-based modeling. But, I suspect, the gains are coming in applying new dynamic mathematical techniques, not in extending comparative static techniques to real-world problems. That application of new techniques to real-world problems so that they fit is an art, and in the future I see significant gains of trade from discussion of literary and mathematical artists.

THE THEME OF THIS BOOK: ARTIPHOBIA

This book is a continuation of the themes of the *Garbagemen* book but it narrows in the debate to focus on the artiphobia element in economists. It represents the evolution of my thinking about the role of economists over the last ten years. It has a bit more methodology in it than the previous book—not the methodology with a capital M, where you get lost in philosophy—but methodology with a small m—discussions of how economists actually go about their work, and where they get their directions from.

Now, to a non-economist, to say that economics is an art, and a good economist is an artist, may sound like a compliment; I certainly mean it as such. But I know many economists will not take it that way. To say that economics is an art goes against the grain of their thinking. They're scientists, which conveys, to them, a sense of precision and clarity. Artists are mushy. Sociologists might be artists; economists surely aren't.

There's been tons of material written on science and art, and I have no intention of going deeply into that literature. From my reading, it quickly becomes more mumbo jumbo than any economics paper. For me, art and science blend into one, both trying to gain a sense of understanding of the world around us. Art, for me, means using one's intuition to gain insight, and imagination in expressing the insights one has gained through the best means possible. Purposeful people are naturally artists.

There are a variety of ways of gaining insight and of storing insights. Science is one of them. Standard science, for me, means a particular type of data compression—storing up insights as efficiently as possible in a mathematical model and conveying those insights to others.

Standard science has been enormously successful in a number of areas, and a variety of sub-branches of science have developed. But there are areas where standard science has been unsuccessful, where empirical verification is difficult to do because of limits on experiments and because no neat models have been found. The data doesn't arrange itself easily into simplified models. Those areas where standard science has not been especially successful generally fall in the area of complex systems—systems which have not been reducible to the simple equations of models, because the interactions are too many, the dynamics are non-linear and beyond specification by simple equations. Unfortunately, economics, as with the other social sciences, is one of those areas.

I've had a hard time convincing many economists that they should be comfortable with the "artist" title. In fact, although I've been arguing with the view for some twenty years now, I'd say that artiphobia in the profession is as rampant now as it was when I started. Why do I keep on harping on it?

Because I think economics is important, and how economists go about doing economics makes a difference to our lives.

If reality were simple, there would be no need for art in science. Art deals with that part of reality that we do not fully understand—that we are not able to compress into a formula or model. When science was young, almost all of reality was dealt with through art—stories, myths, painting, and grunts, which conveyed insights from one individual to another. Grunts, as a way of conveying a representation of the real world, get boring after a while, as do myths, paintings, and songs; they've conveyed what they have to convey, and thus we started to compress our understanding into more precise formulations, generally structured around mathematics. Standard science was born and it was an art form. The development of a new mathematical expression is beautiful, and as artistic as Rembrandt's painting or Mozart's music.

The success of standard science created a worshipping of science that went a bit too far. Standard science was to be applied to everything. But it didn't accommodate everything, and before science could expand to new areas, it had to develop new methods and techniques, something it is only now doing.

Economics is one of those areas where standard science has not been too successful, and the question is how to go about discussing policy where standard science does not fit—where empirical testing is limited, and where simple laws do not seem to be forthcoming even when empirical testing can be done.

My answer is to emphasize the necessity of an artistic side of policy analysis to complement the scientific. The decision I have come to is to reach out to one's artistic side and draw inferences as best one can while incorporating those aspects of the problem that the models cannot handle. This approach is a combination of art and science. To be successful it requires us to be humble— to admit our limitations, and not to present scientific economic arguments for more than what they are, which often is a sense based on highly limited data.

DISCUSSION OF THE ESSAYS

The following twelve chapters (divided into six parts) are essays that I wrote over the past ten years that develop these themes.

Milton Friedman plays a central role in Part I (Chapters 1 and 2) because I see him as a pivotal person in guiding the profession into its current state. He did so through his work on methodology, through example, and through the force of his personality.

Chapter 1 discusses the philosophical foundations for approaching economic policy as an art, and for differentiating it from positive economics. It presents what, to me, is an amusing irony. When Milton Friedman wrote the paper, "The Theory of Positive Economics," that became the foundation of the modern economic policy approach—dividing economics into positive and normative economics—he referred to a book by J.N. Keynes (the father of J.M. Keynes) on *The Scope and Method of Economics*. Friedman remarked that Keynes' work provided the foundation for the positive/normative distinction that he made famous. But there was one problem with this claim. Keynes provided a *tripartite* division of economics—into positive economics, normative economics, and the *art of economics*, with the art of economics including almost all of applied policy. Milton Friedman lost the art of economics from the analysis.

The reason the above story is ironic is discussed in Chapter 2. It argues that Milton Friedman, more than any other modern economist, practiced the art of economics. He eschewed mathematics when others were totally into it, he avoided general equilibrium analysis when it was all the rage, and he kept a policy focus in his work. Had he advertised the fact that he was an artist, and argued that his actual approach, not his stated approach, was the approach one should use to do policy work in economics, the profession today would be fundamentally different than it is, and much better for it.

Part II (Chapters 3 and 4) is devoted to a discussion of the appropriate methodology for the art of economics, and how current economics does not follow it. Chapter 3 proposes some explicit rules for the art of economics, and contrasts those rules with the unwritten rules of applied economics for academics. Chapter 4, written with former Federal Reserve Governor J. Dewey Daane, applies the argument to a subfield of economics—monetary policy. It follows up on a theme from the *Garbagemen* book, suggesting that practitioners have long been doing the art of economics, but that academics often get lost in theory that does not have the necessary institutional foundation. It suggests that economics would be a much more useful guide to monetary policy if academic economists did less high theory and more applied work based on the actual operational details of monetary policy.

Part III (Chapters 5 and 6) deals with teaching economics as an art rather than as a science. In Chapter 5, I argue that teaching economics involves telling stories. Unfortunately, the stories we tell in principles courses are far more boring than they need to be because we are trying to teach a modeling technique as well as teaching the story. Thus, we cannot teach students the story that high-level economists are dealing with; instead we are forced to teach stories we don't believe because they can be related to tractable, principles-level models. The example I give in that chapter is the growth theory we teach, but the argument is more general and could have been related to other areas as well.

Chapter 6 deals with Keynesian economics. Recently, Keynesian economics has been down played in the texts, and replaced with an emphasis on growth and Classical economics. This chapter looks at the reasons for giving up Keynesian economics and comes out firmly in favor of teaching Keynesian economics—not as the definite model of the economy as it was once taught, but as one of the many models that, at times, captures the aspects of the economy that we know. I argue that principles books, in their attempt to simplify, are presenting economic knowledge as more certain than it is, and are thereby giving up teaching the economic method, and concentrating on teaching what the policy answers are. That goes against the methodology of the art of economics.

Part IV (Chapters 7 and 8) consists of two autobiographical essays. I include them because they give one a sense of the economics profession, and what happens to an economist who does not follow the standard track. In Chapter 7, I discuss the question: How do I work? In it I explain that my work follows a random path that is determined by my asking why, and searching for an answer that satisfies me intuitively. This intuitive sense of satisfaction from work is, in my view, the essence of the line of demarcation between art and science. I discuss the relationship between my approach and the MIT and Chicago approaches, and how mine doesn't fit either. I also recount how, given that view, I would have left the economics profession, as many economics graduate students with similar views did, but how I remained in the profession and prospered by a fortuitous set of events, and a lot of help from some older economists who were artists in their own right.

Chapter 8 provides my suggestions for how someone who agrees that economics should be an art can survive in the profession. In it I discuss my rules for good teaching and good research, and how I believe the two must overlap. I then suggest that the key to surviving in the profession is to find an acceptable compromise between one's ideals and the institutional incentives embodied in the reality of the job market. I conclude by arguing that one must be firm in deciding what one's ultimate goal is, but that one's work must fit the institutional environment. After one has become successful, one can work to change the institutional environment.

Part V (Chapters 9 and 10) looks at the effect on the profession of its current artiphobia. Chapter 9 recounts the profession's response to the Commission on Graduate Economic Education (COGEE) Report. COGEE was set up partially in response to Klamer's and my earlier study of the problems in graduate economic education. In the first chapter in this part, I give the background to the COGEE report and recount its key findings. I then discuss the response of the profession to the Commission's report. The title of the chapter, "Sounds of Silence," summarizes that response. At the end of the chapter I then give my personal view of the current state of the profession, and suggest a proposal for changes in graduate economics education. I am under no illusion that my proposal will soon be implemented, but I believe such specific proposals direct those in the profession who agree with me to thinking about where change might be made.

Chapter 10 looks at the impact of artiphobia on the profession. In it I argue that there is not enough disagreement among economists on the big issues and too much agreement on the models that we use. I also argue that the profession's discrimination against artists is self-reinforcing and that fewer and fewer artists are entering the profession. As that happens the profession loses diversity and, with it, much of its vibrancy.

Part VI (Chapters 11 and 12) deals with the future of economics, and is slightly more optimistic about the profession than the earlier essays. Chapter 11 deals with the changes that have occurred in the profession because of advances in mathematics. I argue that modern economics is no longer neoClassical economics; it is broader in its approach and in its dealing with issues than was neoclassical economics. Because of these changes, many of the critics' complaints about economics do not hit home. Modern economics is the economics of the applied policy model. This chapter reiterates my call in the *Garbagemen* book for critics of economics to stop taking easy potshots at the profession and to deal with what is really out there.

The final chapter, Chapter 12, explores what I believe economics will be like fifty years from now. It is written from the perspective of someone looking back from 2050. (So they improved longevity.) It argues that there will have been enormous changes in the structure of the profession and the content of economics. In 2050, I predict, economics will be thought of as a science of a complex system, and that simulation models and agent-based models will replace supply and demand as the workhorse of applied policy models.

CONCLUSION

I concluded in the *Garbagemen* book by arguing that my consideration of the profession is not a statement of cynical defeatism; it is the exact opposite, and it makes sense to conclude this introduction the same way. If a discipline changes, it is because of informed complaints about what the discipline is doing and because of what critics of the discipline are doing. I see my challenges as part of the process through which the invisible hand of truth operates. If some members of the profession view those challenges as correct, the pressure for changes will increase. There's been some change in the profession over the last ten years and I hope I've played a small role. This book is written with the hope of fostering further positive change.

NOTES

1. There are twenty schools in the top ten because there are multiple rankings. A school chooses the ranking that ranks it highest.
2. CSWEP annual report 1999.
3. See footnote 1 and page 1.
4. Recently, econometricians have been coming to grips with these problems. See Peter Kennedy (2000).

PART I

How the Art of Economics was Lost

1.   The Lost Art of Economics*

Economists generally divide economics into two distinct categories— positive and normative—but how applied economics fits within these categories is unclear. This chapter argues that applied economics belongs in neither normative nor positive economics; instead it belongs in a third category—the art of economics. Currently, many economists are trying to use a methodology appropriate for positive economics to guide their applied work, work that properly belongs in the art of economics.

This three-part distinction is not mine, but dates back to a classic book, *The Scope and Method of Political Economy* (1891) by the father of John Maynard Keynes, John Neville Keynes. What is particularly ironic about losing the art of economics is that it was lost while in plain sight. By that I mean that in the United States at least, the entrenchment of the positive/normative distinction dates back to Milton Friedman's (1953) "Methodology of Positive Economics," where Friedman cites J.N. Keynes as his reference for the positive/normative distinction. But Friedman actually quotes J.N. Keynes' discussion of a *three-part* distinction. Friedman writes (p. 3):

> In his admirable book on *The Scope and Method of Political Economy,* John Neville Keynes distinguishes among "a positive science . . . a body of systematized knowledge concerning what is; a normative or regulative science . . . a body of systematized knowledge discussing criteria of what ought to be . . . ; an art . . . a system of rules for the attainment of a given end"; comments that "confusion between them is common and has been the source of many mischievous errors"; and urges the importance of "recognizing a distinct positive science of political economy."

Friedman's essay (and most post-Friedman economic methodological work) discusses the methodology appropriate for positive economics. But using Keynes' tripartite division, most economists' work does not belong in positive economics. If one accepts Keynes' three-part division, Friedman's and most subsequent methodological discussions are not relevant to a major portion of economists' work. Friedman placed Keynes' tripartite distinction in the open and then he lost it.[1]

In his book, Keynes argued that economists' failure to distinguish the art of economics as a separate branch from positive and normative economics would lead to serious problems. One hundred years later, he has turned out to be clairvoyant.

SCIENCE, ART, AND APPLIED ECONOMICS

Keynes placed his discussion of the art of economics under the heading "Applied Economics" (p. 55). According to Keynes, positive economics is the study of what is and the way the economy works; it is pure science, not applied economics. Normative economics is the study of what should be; it is not applied economics. The art of economics is applied economics. It relates the lessons learned in positive economics to the normative goals determined in normative economics.

The methodology Keynes finds appropriate for the art of economics is fundamentally different from the methodology he finds appropriate for normative economics or for positive economics. He wrote:

> [F]ew practical problems admit of complete solution on economic grounds alone ... [W]hen we pass, for instance, to problems of taxation, or to problems that concern the relations of the State with trade and industry, or to the general discussion of communistic and socialistic schemes—it is far from being the case that economic considerations hold the field exclusively. Account must also be taken of ethical, social, and political considerations that lie outside the sphere of political economy regarded as a science [p. 34] ...

> We are, accordingly, led to the conclusion ... that a definitive art of political economy, which attempts to lay down absolute rules for the regulation of human conduct, will have vaguely defined limits, and be largely non-economic in character [p. 83] ...

> The main point to notice is that the endeavor to merge questions of what ought to be with questions of what is tends to confuse, not only economic discussions themselves, but also discussions about economic method. The relative value to be attached to different methods of investigation is very different, according as we take the ethical and practical standpoint, or the purely scientific standpoint. Thus it would be generally agreed that, in dealing with practical questions, an abstract method of treatment avails less and carries us much less far than when we are dealing with theoretical questions. In other words, in dealing with the former class of questions, we are to a greater extent dependent upon history and inductive generalization.

> Again, while economic uniformities and economic precepts are both, in many cases, relative to particular states of society, the general relativity of the latter may be affirmed with less qualification than that of the former. "Political economy," says Sir James Steuart, and by this he means the art of political economy, "in each country must necessarily be different"; and, so far as practical questions are concerned, this is hardly too strong a statement. On such questions there is nearly always something to be said on both sides, so that practical decisions can be arrived at only by weighing counter-arguments one against another. But the relative force of these argument is almost certain to vary with varying conditions. We are not here denying the relativity of economic theorems, but merely affirming

the greater relativity of economic precepts. Unless the distinction between theorems and precepts is carefully borne in mind, the relativity of the former is likely to be over-stated [pp. 63–65].

As these quotations show, Keynes saw applied economics as the art of economics and believed that the appropriate methodology for the art of economics is different from the appropriate methodology for positive economics. The profession has not followed Keynes' division and, as he warned would happen, the distinction between precepts and theorems has often been over stated, and implications from economic theory have been drawn which do not follow, causing others to overstate the relativity of the theories of economic science. Explicitly recognizing the art of economics would make a major difference in the methodological conventions of economics.

THE ART OF ECONOMICS AND POSITIVE ECONOMICS

Positive economics suffers from the lack of an art of economics because, if a separate art is not delineated, positive economic inquiry faces pressures to have policy relevance, which is constraining to imaginative scientific inquiry. Positive economics is abstract thinking about abstract problems which might someday have some relevance, but immediate relevance is simply a side issue of no concern to the positive researcher. Imagine, for example, if theoretical physics were required to maintain policy relevance. Einstein's thought experiments would have been seen as a waste of time.

Few observers would deny that most economic inquiry today is abstract thinking about abstract problems. But abstract is not necessarily imaginative. Much of the current abstract thinking is the mundane application of technique to precisely defined problems; such work seldom leads to significant advances in science. If positive economics were freed from policy relevance, imagination would be enhanced.

THE ART OF ECONOMICS AND TODAY'S APPLIED ECONOMICS

The current version of applied economics suffers from the lack of an art of economics because it feels compelled to use methodology imported from positive economics. Thus, most current applied work in economics initially employs a formalistic method of argumentation and exposition which leads to exact results.[2] The formalistic results are then modified by political and sociological dimensions (or, at least, a sentence at the end of the work states that the results need to be so modified). These dimensions are addenda, made after the formal analysis is complete.

This sequencing loses interconnections between the various dimensions and leads to much work that is needlessly precise. The reason is analogous to the law of significant digits—the results of an analysis can only be as exact as the least precise part of the analysis. Since the sociological and political dimensions are extraordinarily imprecise, making applied economic theory precise adds nothing to the precision of the final conclusion.

For example, economists have analyzed the optimal tariff and the optimal tax and have come up with enormously precise results (usually specified in long equations). These economists agree that before the analysis can be applied to the real world, the imprecise historical, institutional, political, social, and distributional dimensions must be added back to the analysis. But if the final policy recommendation is no more precise than these dimensions, the economic precision has served no purpose. Actually, it may have served a negative purpose since some interconnections among dimensions are likely lost in the process.

Many economists implicitly think of applied work of the type I am suggesting as subjective and normative; they implicitly equate positive economic analysis with objective analysis. That's wrong. All economic analysis—positive, normative and art—should be as objective as possible. Good applied economic work tells people how to achieve the goals they want to achieve as effectively as they can. No normative judgments about those goals need be made, and the analysis should remain objective. Even normative economics should be objective. It should discuss society's goals, and the reasons why these goals should be followed. It may be harder to maintain objectivity in the art of economics, but that simply suggests that one must work harder.

THE ART OF ECONOMICS AND EMPIRICAL ECONOMICS

Applying the methodology of the art of economics to empirical work would also bring about significant changes. Most empirical work done by academic economists is currently very formal, technical, econometric analysis. Often the researchers' knowledge of the institutions they are studying is limited to computer printouts of large data sets. Empirical tests are also formal and results are expected to fall within 95 percent or 99 percent confidence intervals. This might be appropriate for empirical work in positive economics; it is not appropriate to empirical work in the art of economics.

In the art of economics, because of the interconnection of sociological and political dimensions of the problem, precise tests are impossible. Judgment dependent on institutional and historical information is required. This means that in the art of economics a wide range of observation and empirical exploration is appropriate. Often simple statistics, tables, charts, and case studies are the appropriate modes of expression for empirical work in the art of economics.

The purpose of empirical work in the art of economics is not to test theories; it is to apply theories to real-world problems. The appropriate methodology for such applications involves sociological and political observations and, to stay within the confines of precision established by the law of significant digits, is generally not precise.

Empirical work in positive economics should be designed to test whether a theory should be tentatively accepted; such empirical tests may have little or no relevance in applying a theory to a real-world problem. Empirical work in the art of economics should be designed to apply a theory by adding back the contextual reality. The two types of empirical work are fundamentally different. Current practice does not differentiate between the two.

THE ART OF ECONOMICS AND NORMATIVE ECONOMICS

Reintroducing the art of economics would free normative economics from dealing with economic policy and allow a deeper consideration of what policy goals are appropriate. The art of economics would accept some set of goals determined in normative economics, and discuss how to achieve those goals in the real world, given the insights of positive economics.

RESHAPING ECONOMIC EDUCATION

Explicit recognition that most economists' work falls under the classification of the art of economics would change the way economics is taught at both the undergraduate and graduate level. The appropriate methodology for the art of economics is much broader, more inclusive, and far less technical than the methodological approach for positive economics that underlies current teaching practices. The art of economics requires knowledge of institutions, of social, political, and historical phenomena, and the ability to use available data in a reasonable way in discussing real-world economic issues. These aspects of economic knowledge have been purged from the graduate curriculum in economics. Only 3 percent of the graduate students at top universities stated that having a thorough knowledge of the economy is very important to succeeding as an economist, while 68 percent of them said that knowledge was unimportant (Klamer and Colander, 1990). If economists accepted that the appropriate methodological conventions were those of the art of economics, graduate training would change significantly. Most students would be taught to interpret, use, and apply theory, not to develop it.

The blurring of the distinction between positive and normative economics occurs early in students' careers. Introductory textbooks commonly divide economics into positive and normative, and then conclude that anything involving a value judgment belongs in the normative category (for example, Samuelson and Nordhaus, 1989, pp. 10–11; McConnell and Brue, 1990, p. 6). Since any statement about what policy should be followed must necessarily involve a normative goal, these definitions place all policy considerations outside of positive economics.

Having so classified economics, these books then proceed to discuss economic policy issues, focusing on economic efficiency and giving the impression that discussions of efficiency belong in positive economics. However, achieving economic efficiency is not an end in itself, but is a debatable, normative goal which often will conflict with other normative goals society might have.

Only if teachers of economics introduce the third division—the art of economics—will the distinction between normative and positive economics become clear. Separating out the art of economics allows one to point out that objectivity in the art of economics is not achieved by avoiding value judgments, but, rather, by making clear what are the value judgments upon which one is basing the policy recommendation.

THE ART OF ECONOMICS AND DEBATES ABOUT POLICY

Economists raised with the positive/normative distinction tend to argue, as the Samuelson and Nordhaus textbook put it, "The major disagreements among economists, however, lie in normative areas." However, if economists are being objective, either their own normative views should not enter into their analyses, or they should state what those normative views are, and why those normative views should be used. In either case, it is difficult to see normative areas as the source of disagreement. I believe many or most of the debates about economic policy are not debates about normative issues; they are debates about how best to achieve an agreed-upon normative end.

Friedman (1953) was clearer about the reasons for differences among economists' policy recommendations. He states (p. 4):

I venture the judgment, however, that currently in the Western world, and especially in the United States, differences about economic policy among disinterested citizens derive predominantly from different predictions about the economic consequences of taking action—differences that in principle can be eliminated by the progress of positive economics—rather than from fundamental differences in basic values, differences about which men can ultimately only fight.

The problem with this statement is the inserted phrase, "differences that in principle can be eliminated by the progress of positive economics." This phrase assumes that policy conclusions flow directly from positive economics. However, as Keynes argued, the art of economics is contextual and as much dependent on non-economic political, social, institutional, and historical judgments as it is on economics.[3] Thus, advances in positive economics generally will not help settle policy differences among economists because those policy differences result primarily from different judgments about political and social dimensions of policy implementation, not about differences in underlying theory.

CONCLUSION

Recognizing that what most economists do belongs in the category of the art of economics, and taking seriously the appropriate methodology for that category, would fundamentally change the economics profession. But as a realist, I recognize that few practicing economists will heed this or any other methodological discussion; they do what they do.

However, historians of thought do take methodology seriously and this chapter is a criticism of much of the economic methodological literature. That literature has refined the methodology of positive economics ad infinitum, but those refinements are irrelevant to most economists because most economists don't do positive economics. They do applied economics, and the relevant category for applied economics is the art of economics. Keynes had definite views of what the appropriate methodology for the art of economics is; I agree with him. Many in the profession may disagree, but that is where the methodological debate should focus. The economics profession is overdue to begin a serious discussion on the appropriate methodology for the art of economics.

NOTES

* I would like to thank Roger Backhaus, Mark Blaug, Larry Boland, Daniel Hammond, Thomas Mayer, Cordelia Reimers, Carl Shapiro, Joseph Stiglitz, and Timothy Taylor for helpful comments on earlier drafts of this chapter.

1. A likely reason why Keynes' tripartite distinction was not central to Friedman's essay is that the reference to J.N. Keynes was a late addition to the essay. According to Daniel Hammond (March 1991), early drafts of Friedman's essay did not include any positive/normative distinction, let alone a tripartite one. In fact, the term "positive economics" did not make it into the title until the final draft.
2. A majority of graduating Ph.D.s classify themselves as "applied theorists." Applied theory is exactly what the art of economics is, and according to Keynes it is largely non-economic in character. Yet Ph.D. theses are generally required to follow a positivist methodology.
3. Larry Boland (1991) makes a similar point about this problem with Friedman's methodology.

2. Is Milton Friedman an Artist or a Scientist?*

Milton Friedman is a brilliant economist. He has significantly influenced microeconomic policy, macroeconomic policy, and economic methodology. Despite this influence, he is not seen as one of the fathers of modern economics. In fact, he is seen by many young economists as outside the mainstream in both methodology and in theory, even as the mainstream is supporting and adopting many of Friedman's policy proposals that it viewed as radical and outside the mainstream when Friedman first presented them. Underlying this majority assessment of his theoretical and methodological approach are the views that (1) his work is flawed by ideological biases, and (2) his particular brand of Marshallian economics is outdated, long ago superseded by modern Walrasian economics and advanced econometric techniques.[1] In the eyes of the mainstream, Friedman is passé.

In responding to these criticisms, Friedman's many supporters argue that he has been misunderstood, that he does not have an ideological bias, and that he has not been unscientific; they contend that his work is not obsolete but remains directly relevant. For example, in a recent article (1993a) and book (1993b) Thomas Mayer argues that in the context of its time, Milton Friedman's "The Methodology of Positive Economics" was a "plea for a positivistic interplay of theory and observation." Giving Friedman's essay and approach a soft reading and casting it in a Mayerian reasonableness that removes its sharp edges and inherent pro-market biases that so excited critics, Mayer argues that one would expect that economists who adhere to the broad empiricist tradition of economics would applaud its influence (p. 221). Similarly, Abraham Hirsch and Neil De Marchi (1990) recently completed a sympathetic analysis of Friedman's work.

In this chapter I consider these differing views of Friedman's supporters and of the mainstream. I propose an explanation for the differences and a modified interpretation of how Friedman's work should be viewed. Specifically, I argue that Friedman, like Alfred Marshall before him, tried to straddle a fence between policy and logical-deductive theory, combining the artistic science of the historical and institutional school with the logical-deductive science of economics under a single category—which Friedman called positive economics. This combination worked for Marshall, in part because in

Marshall's day formal logical-deductive economic analysis was still in its in-
fancy, and so didn't need to be separated from applied policy economics, and
in part because of Marshall's proclivity to avoid taking strong policy stands,
hence avoiding normative issues in the art of economics.

The combination did not work for Friedman for two reasons. First, by
Friedman's time, with the work of economists such as John Hicks and Paul
Samuelson becoming widely known, formal theoretical work had generalized
theoretical economic insights sufficiently so that the Marshallian straddle—
the attempt to combine theory and practice—no longer made sense, if it ever
did. Second, whereas Marshall was hesitant to make strong policy statements
on specific issues, keeping his engine of analysis focused on broad policy
issues, Friedman wasn't; Friedman combined a normative belief in individual
liberty with his intuitive sense of theory to arrive at strong policy views with
which many economists did not agree. Taking specific account of normative
beliefs (beyond Pareto optimality) is a necessary part of any meaningful applied policy work, or the artistic branch of economic science; it has no place
in the logical-deductive positive branch of economics.

The economist to whom Friedman attributed this positive/normative distinction, J.N. Keynes, provided an alternative to the Marshallian straddle that
could have been a way out for Friedman. That way out was a separation of
economics into three categories: positive economics, normative economics,
and the art of economics. But, ironically, after citing Keynes' tripartite distinction, Friedman proceeded to discuss economic methodology as if there
were a two-part division. By not distinguishing between the methodology
applicable for applied policy work and the methodology applicable for theoretical development work as Keynes had done, Friedman furthered methodological confusion in economics, as Keynes had argued such a failure to distinguish between the two would do.

Since this division of economics is central to my argument, let me briefly
summarize it.

POSITIVE ECONOMICS

In Keynes' tripartite division, positive economics is a highly abstract logical
deductive branch of economics; it is concerned with understanding the workings of the economy for the sake of understanding; it has no direct concern
about policy implications.[2] Its appropriate methodology is debatable, but a
case can be made for the current vogue—a highly abstract, unworldly, approach in which assumptions are unrealistic. It is to such an approach that
Friedman's F-Twist is most defensible. Empirical work in positive economics
is designed to test theories formally and possibly falsify them; if one can do

so, one arrives at an economic law. Empirical work in positive economics has nothing to do with applying those theories to real-world problems. Almost all recent methodological discussions in economics have been directed at this branch of economics, as if it were the only branch of economics.

NORMATIVE ECONOMICS

Normative economics is a philosophical inquiry into the goals of economies. It considers questions such as: What should an economy be attempting to achieve? How does one reconcile differing valuations of individuals? What moral limitations is it appropriate to place on values? Thus, normative economics is a philosophical inquiry directly focused on values.

The appropriate scope and method for normative economics was scarcely considered by J.N. Keynes, and has been little discussed since his time. Its method could be highly formal, as in much of social choice theory, or heuristic, as in Henry Simons' consideration of altruism. Its scope could be limited to economic issues, but could also be much broader. In either case, it is the branch of economics that interrelates with philosophy and ethics and that provides insights into the goals of economics.

THE ART OF ECONOMICS: APPLIED POLICY ECONOMICS

The art of economics provides the connection between positive economics and normative economics. It takes the insights learned in the positive economics and the goals determined in the normative branch of economics and analyses how to realistically best achieve those goals. It concerns real-world solutions to real-world problems. It is to positive economics what engineering is to pure science. As I argue in Chapter 1, its scope is necessarily broad; it must relate the laws of abstract theory to the real world; whatever considerations relevant to real-world policy that were ruled out in normative and positive economics must be added back in. For example, if the scope of positive economics is limited to economic issues, then the relevant sociological and political issues must be added in. Normative sensibilities, as well as explicit normative goals, must similarly be added to the insights of positive theory to arrive at policy prescriptions.

Whether or not the art of economics should be classified as part of the science of economics is not at issue. Science is many things to many different people. Thus, one can think of the art of economics as the "policy branch of science" and of positive economics as the "logical-deductive branch of science." The point at issue is whether applied policy work should explicitly be subject to the same set of methodological rules as work designed to develop and understand the logical implications of theories. My argument is that it should not be. Separation is necessary to avoid methodological confusion.

An example of a minimum wage law may make the distinction clearer: positive economics—logical-deductive theory—tells us very little about a minimum wage law. It simply tells us that employment will be redirected away from those activities subject to minimum wages into other activities not subject to a minimum wage. Based on positive theory alone, economics has nothing to say about whether a minimum wage law makes sense, and should be supported.

It does, however, provide a structure for judging minimum wage laws, incorporating judgments about issues, such as whether the redirected activities were undesirable, and, if so, how undesirable; what the redistributive effects have often been; and how people's attitudes are affected by that redirection. After incorporating these issues, many economists oppose minimum wage laws. That conclusion is what Keynes called a precept. It does not follow from theory, but is arrived at from a mixture of judgment and theory. All precepts belong in the art of economics, not in the positive science of economics.

Empirical work in the art of economics is quite different from empirical work in positive economics. Empirical work in the art of economics is unconcerned with testing the theory as true or not; it accepts the theoretical insights developed in positive economics. What empirical work in the art of economics is concerned with is whether or not the theory fits the real world. That means adding back the relevant elements of the real-world economy that the deductive positive science has removed. Doing so can involve significant statistical and econometric work, but the purpose of that work is not to test theories to see if they are true, but instead to sift information from the data, information that is to be integrated with one's direct knowledge of the institutions so that the researcher can come to a policy recommendation based on the best available evidence.

Adding such realism requires judgment and the integration of quantifiable and non-quantifiable data. This integration reduces the degrees of accuracy and, following the law of significant digits, generally leads to highly informal empirical work. It would consider case studies, history, common sense empiricism, and statistical work, including data mining such as vector autoregressions. Since the formal requirements of classical statistical tests will not be met in this statistical work, the results of the tests will not be definitive, but will instead be simply a guide to the applied policy researcher in coming to a decision. Integrating these various forms of empirical data requires an intuitive sensibility. In the art of economics one is continually asking: Does the result make educated intuitive sense? (An educated intuitive sense differs from a lay person's intuitive sense because it assumes that the person is aware of the insights found in logical-deductive science. For example, it would involve the person knowing the equivalency of the income and excise tax, and all second and n-best arguments. These insights would be counterintuitive for the lay person.) Thus, in the art of economics, application is key and instrumentalism fits in perfectly. The purpose of the art of economics is application to real-world problems.

FRIEDMAN, MARSHALL, AND THE ART OF ECONOMICS

Keynes argued that it was necessary to use separate methodologies in developing theory—in positive economics, and in applying theory—in the art of economics. That separation of art and positive science would allow normative beliefs to play a key role in influencing policy, and would separate economic precepts—informal judgments that economists make, judgments that are debatable and based on a broad sensibility—from economic laws that follow from logical-deductive theory. The Marshallian straddle, which Friedman followed, combined the two, and thereby led to "confusion" and "mischievous errors," precisely as Keynes said they would.

Had Friedman been faced with a choice of doing art—applied policy analysis —or positive economic analysis as it is currently practiced, I believe he would have unequivocally decided on applied policy economics, arguing that such applied work should be the primary concern of economists. (In fact, he might well argue that what I am calling positive economic analysis is not worth doing.) Instead he chose a methodological position that avoided that choice. He implicitly argued that theoretical analysis and applied policy analysis need not be separated. The profession followed his lead. An economist could do both theoretical analysis and applied policy analysis simultaneously. The problem this caused was that both were subjected to the same methodological rules, which quickly became the rules that science had developed to govern the choice of theories.

This combining of the art and developmental theory science, and their joint use of positive methodological rules, gave strong impetus for more and more resources to be devoted to theoretical analysis, and for fewer and fewer resources to go for applied policy analysis, since good applied policy work did not fit the positivistic methodology of science as it was then interpreted. The result is the current state of academic economics, which gives major emphasis to logical-deductive theory, is cynical about empirical work, and gives short shrift to history and institutions.

This is not to say that there is nothing called applied economics currently being done in academic economic research. But it is to say that much of this so-called applied policy work does not incorporate real-world complications with theory in a realistic way. It does not provide a link between positive economics and normative economics, but is instead simply a recharacterization of formal models to a slightly different setting. A previously developed technique or model is "applied" to a different area, and the formal equilibrium solution is arrived at. For example, a general maximization model exists that shows the equilibrium conditions that would exist if individuals maximized subject to certain constraints. This maximization model can be formally adapted to urban economics, health economics, public finance, and so on, but in each case the general structure of the solution remains the same.

Such formal adaptations are the result of placing applied policy economics in the same category as logical-deductive theory. These formal adaptations look like impressive scientific models, but are of little use to most real-world policy makers, and are best identified as game-playing—useful as exercises for teaching and understanding the implications of the generalized model, but not especially helpful in applying economic insights to real-world problems. The tendency to call such pedagogical exercises "applied economics" has led to sterility and complaints that much economics is irrelevant.

I am not arguing that economists who are doing this applied policy research are not behaving rationally. They are; they are responding to institutional incentives within the academic community for publication. What I am saying is that the incentives in existing academic institutions are not toward doing true applied policy work. True applied policy work quickly becomes too institutionally specialized. It must assume its reader has a much higher awareness of those institutional issues than the readership of a general journal has. True applied policy work might lead to internal policy papers but it is highly unlikely to lead to large numbers of journal articles. That is why we so seldom see government and policy institution authors of journal articles.

True applied policy work will not have a wide audience among academic economists (who are the primary readers and editors of those journals, publication in which counts for tenure). Pedagogical exercises that are useful for teaching or are self-referential to other academic articles have a much broader readership among academic economists. Thus, given the current academic institutions, it is only rational for academic economists to initially address other academic economists, not policy makers. Once one has an academic reputation and tenure one can do more meaningful applied policy work. But that work leads to fewer articles and less recognition among academic economists.

As I discuss elsewhere (Colander, 1991b), the reasons why the economics profession has gone the way it has involve incentives and the institutional structure of the academic profession. Promotion and success depend on publication and if one can get a publication for doing an exercise that is useful for teaching the central elements of positive theory, the costs of learning those insights are reduced. Friedman is a strong opponent of this current state (Mayer, 1993a), but ironically that state is due, in part, to the profession's acceptance of Friedman's methodological position that made applied policy analysis subject to the same methodological rules that govern the development theory branch of economics.

ECONOMISTS, FRIEDMAN'S METHODOLOGY, AND THE ART OF ECONOMICS

Most economists care little about methodology; they're interested in getting on with what they do, not in talking about what they do. This has led a new group of economic methodologists to discuss methodology in relation to how economists do economics rather than what they say about methodology (Daniel Hammond, 1991a, 1992; Abraham Hirsch and Neil De Marchi, 1990; and Thomas Mayer 1993a, 1993b). Their approach is to study the works of economists and to draw out methodological principles from those works, rather than to look at what the economist writes about methodology. It is their work that has led to renewed interest in Friedman's and Marshall's methodology. Because their work does such a good job in considering Friedman's methodology, in this chapter I do not try to analyze Friedman's approach or work in detail. This chapter presumes a familiarity with this new methodological work, which provides an appropriately sympathetic interpretation of Friedman's methodology, making the points that (1) Friedman was a Marshallian; (2) Friedman was not a philosopher of science; (3) Friedman's work is coherent and consistent if one concentrates on Friedman's actual economic work, rather than on his methodological essay (giving his methodological essay a soft, rather than hard, reading). I agree with each of those three conclusions.

While I admire this new work, and find it of more relevance to economists than the more esoteric philosophical methodological literature, it remains tangential to most economists' concerns. Most economists want to get on with their work without thinking about the broader questions of whether their work has meaning and fits into a meaningful discipline that is uncovering, if not truth, at least insights into the workings of the economy. Most economists implicitly believe the following: Just as a person who continually questions the meaning of life will probably be led into a catatonic daze, so, too, will an economist who continually questions the underlying methodology. Their position is: Let us get on with our work; let us follow the institutional incentives for tenure, promotion, and success.

There is a logic to this position. Academic institutional incentives are strong, and methodologists should be under no illusion that anything they write or say is going to change that. That said, there is a certain satisfaction that comes from believing that one's work has relevance, or, at least, from not having to directly face questions of its relevance. That is what is so comforting for the normal academic economist about the positive/normative distinction: economists are extending science which, by nature, is abstract and esoteric—studying economics for the sake of understanding the economy. Non-economists don't appreciate economists' work simply because they don't appreciate science.

Thus, the methodological conceptions that academic economists have about their discipline play a role in determining what they do, especially when considered jointly in relation to the set of incentives that they face for job promotion and tenure. They justify their work to themselves with the belief that it is contributing to the growth of economic science. From day one they hear the positive science methodological prescription: Develop a formal model and formally test it.

In the new methodological literature, it is clear that Friedman's brand of positive economics has a far more complicated methodological prescription underlying it than is captured in what is generally called positive methodology. Friedman's methodology involves intuition, a blending of institutional and theoretical knowledge, and a lack of interest in doing abstract theory.

The reaction of most economists to this new methodological work will, I suspect, be, "So what?" Most economists do not view Friedman as a role model, but rather as an historical figure. Economists' interest is less in how economics has been done by stars in the past than it is in how it should be done. They are interested in prescription, not historical discussion.

In looking for prescription, they continually come back to the prescriptions that they have interpreted as positive economics: develop an abstract formal model and formally test it. The new methodologists nicely show that this was not Friedman's approach. But, as I stated above, it was Friedman's 1953 essays that enshrined the positive/normative distinction in economic textbooks, which is probably the only place where most economists encounter methodological issues. Thus, ironically, the current lack of interest in Friedman's methodology may be due, in part, to Friedman himself.

In their appraisal of Friedman, Hirsch and De Marchi (1990) derive five methodological rules from his work. These rules are the following:

1. Adopt an "outside" view of behavior.
2. Start with observation.
3. Test implications continually.
4. Use the best knowledge available.
5. Do not look for answers "in principle" but address concrete problems.

These are not the methodological rules the economics profession normally thinks of as the rules of positive economics; these rules are not rules for testing to see whether a theory is true, but are instead rules for testing, using common sense, to see if the insights of economic theory are applicable to real-world problems. These rules are very similar to rules I propose for the art of economics in the next chapter, which is why I believe Friedman's work serves as an example of good applied policy economics.[3] Thus, while Friedman's actual methodology is only of historical interest for the science of economics, it is of direct interest for the art of economics.

THE EVOLUTIONARY NATURE OF ECONOMIC METHODOLOGY

In any field there is an ongoing relationship between its applied policy branch and its theoretical development branch. As fields develop the appropriate methodology changes. Thus, just as Marshall argued that the appropriate natural science analogy for economics is evolutionary, so too is the appropriate analogy for methodology.

A field of inquiry almost always begins with applied policy or art researchers studying situations and finding reasonable rules of thumb for dealing with them. As the inquiry continues, certain similarities in answers to problems are found, and artistic generalizations made. Initially these artistic generalizations are heuristic, but as more people consider them, the insights become more and more formalized until someone "picks the oysters," making certain assumptions, showing the essence of the idea in an elegant formal model. In economics most of the oysters were picked in the period from 1930 to 1955, with the work of such economists as Samuelson, Lerner, and Hicks. They carried out the logic of the individual maximization model and strung the pearls of wisdom in general models. These general models convey the implications of economic theory far more efficiently than do artistic generalizations.

Once the general model has been developed, the nature of applied policy economics fundamentally changes. The oysters have been picked; now they need to be shucked, which means that the institutional issues and other assumptions that were put in the back of one's mind are added back in. In short, up until the 1950s, it may have made sense to combine applied policy and theoretical development; after the 1950s it did not. Once one understands the core theory, there is no need to redo the formal theorist's analysis in each area of application. Instead one can use the accepted theory, and deal with the application of the theory—adding back the judgments, and the institutional detail necessary to come to a policy conclusion.

Friedman's methodological essay was written at the cusp of this transition; he picked some theoretical oysters—for example his work on the logical equivalency of an excise and income tax, or his work with Savage on risk preference—but the majority of his work focused on the applied policy. Looking at the majority of his work, one sees it is highly policy oriented. It often uses a heuristic methodology, integrating astute observation with a sense and a feel for the political institutions, a good sense of the implications of the theoretical economic model, and strong normative judgments about the relative importance of liberty for a good society. Judged relative to the methodology of the art of economics, Friedman is a brilliant practitioner.

FRIEDMAN, MARSHALL, AND THE ART OF ECONOMICS

In his writings, Friedman has made it very clear that he sees himself as a Marshallian; he is following in the Marshallian tradition. This is to be contrasted with the Walrasian approach, which is a highly abstract mathematical approach to economics that uses a general equilibrium, rather than a partial equilibrium, framework. The Marshallian method involves the use of a less abstract mathematical approach that keeps assumptions in the back of one's mind and integrates real-world institutions into the analysis, whenever the analysis is applied. Most academic economists today consider themselves Walrasians; Friedman considers himself a Marshallian.

Exactly where Marshall stood on the art of economics is unclear. In early editions of his *Principles*, he argued against a separate art of economics and focused on economics as a science. Marshall's concept of science, however, was not of a logical-deductive science as it is often thought of today. When Marshall and J.N. Keynes were writing, what J.N. Keynes called the art of economics was dominant in the German historical tradition. As discussed in Blaug (1980, p. 82), both Keynes and Marshall were attempting to reconcile the art of economics with the logical-deductive theoretical approach. In his integration Marshall gave short shrift to the "logical-deductive" approach; he combined it with the applied-policy economics. Keynes, on the other hand, left room for that "logical-deductive" branch of economics, and classified it as positive economics, leaving the art of economics as the applied policy branch.

By combining the two branches Marshall tried to forge a theory that could be everything to everyone; that merged supply considerations with demand considerations, applied policy science with pure science, and formalism with non-formalism. Whereas Walras advocated a formalistic general equilibrium, Marshall, the mediator, advocated partial equilibrium. Marshall eschewed mathematics, but simultaneously structured his arguments in the *Principles* so that they could be deduced mathematically; those mathematics were placed in an appendix if they were included at all. He incorporated enormous institutional and historical insights into his *Principles,* but he simultaneously removed "political" from the name of his discipline, calling it economics rather than political economy.

Marshall's argument against art and his focus on economics as science must be understood in the context of the times; when he was writing, economics as a separate discipline did not yet exist. The majority of economists he dealt with talked about policy, not theory. Only a small minority did theory or followed a logical-deductive approach. As he was writing the *Principles,* he was also petitioning Cambridge to set up separate tripos in economics and was very much concerned that the objectivity of economics be maintained (Marshall, 1902). Given his institutional needs, it is not surprising that he combined the art of economics and positive economics, and emphasized the scientific logical-deductive nature of economics.

Despite combining the art and positive branches of economics together, Marshall carefully separated out applied policy work from his analytic work. For example, when he discussed the art of economics in the fourth edition he wrote:

> Of course an economist retains the liberty, common to all the world, of expressing his opinion that a certain course of action is the right one under given circumstances; and if the difficulties of the problem are chiefly economic, he may speak with a certain authority. But on the whole, though the matter is one on which opinions differ, it seems best that he should do so rather in his private capacity, than as claiming to speak with the authority of economic science. (Vol. 11, p. 154)

Consistent with this view, Marshall was extremely hesitant to draw policy conclusions from economic theory. Policy issues—the art of economics— required normative and institutional judgments that had to be added back to the logical-deductive theoretical model. Policy conclusions did not follow from theory alone. What I am arguing is that Marshall's approach to real-world problems much more closely follows what I have suggested is the appropriate methodology of the art of economics than it does what we currently think of as the positive science of economics. For example, while he generally held to the quantity theory of money, he agreed that it would be swamped by other forces in individual cases. Alternatively, consider Marshall's analysis of the taxes that is discussed in Hirsch and De Marchi. They point out that for Marshall the analysis of direct incentive effects was only a starting point of his analysis of taxes (Hirsch and De Marchi, 1990, p. 161). Another example they give is Marshall's consideration of the question of import duties. In that consideration Marshall states a variety of specific questions that need to be answered before one can come to a policy conclusion. They write:

> Marshall operates not as a theorist who sets up his assumptions and then reasons out (to some general conclusions for hypothetical categories of cases), *but as one who actually has to give advice, or make the decision in favor of one tax or another, or for no tax at all* [emphasis supplied]. He cautions frequently against making direct application of the results of simple first-round impact analysis. A prefatory note in his Memorandum, for example, points out that "the incidence of import duties is extremely complex" and he adds: "the indirect are often much more important than the direct effects". . . Marshall also warns that although the exposition to follow is concerned chiefly with "proximate causes and their effects" a student should actually be "endeavoring to probe to the causes of causes." (p. 162)

Finally, Marshall's views changed over time. This is not surprising since Marshall and J.N. Keynes were close friends, and Marshall may have been influenced by Keynes' arguments for separating out an art of economics from positive economics. Between the third (1895) and fourth (1898) editions, a few years after Keynes' book came out, Marshall cut from his *Principles* a paragraph arguing against using the term "art of economics" (vol. 11, p. 154).

ART, SCIENCE, AND THE TEACHING OF ECONOMICS

Both Friedman and Marshall were primarily teachers of economics. Indeed the primary reason why there is any interest in the positive/normative distinction at all is that it is about the only methodological distinction that economics students are taught. That, certainly, is the reason I am interested in it.

The teaching of economics poses additional constraints on the ideas one develops as an economist and, I think, failure to distinguish the pedagogical needs of teaching from the needs of positive economics and the needs of applied policy economics has caused much confusion. Formal modeling of specific cases is often useful for teaching a general model. Formal modeling is also useful in teaching students to approach problems systematically, to separate out analysis from normative judgments. It follows that even if one believes that the art of economics is ultimately what most economists should be doing, and hence what should be taught, one does not necessarily go out and direct students to do applied policy work. One must first convey to students the general insights of the field upon which economists' general sensibility is based. Exercises applying the formal general model to a specific setting are a good way to accomplish this. Doing the particulars teaches one the specifics. They are wonderful teaching exercises, but they are not applied policy economics. Formal models of specific instances are to applied policy economics what exercises are to a sport: necessary to sharpen skills, but not the sport itself.

It follows that to teach students the art of economics, one must teach specific formal models. But if one is teaching these models as a foundation for applied-policy economics, the models must be taught as calisthenics—as an exercise of the students' minds to prepare them to start dealing with the more difficult issues of art.

The needs of models for pedagogical purposes are that they must be challenging, but not too challenging; the models currently taught in introductory and intermediate economics are approximately right for their intended purpose of exercising students' minds. Combining applied policy economics with positive economics has, however, led to a tendency for these exercises of the mind to become more and more elaborate and to create students who are the Charles Atlases of such exercises, but have no training in going beyond such exercises and doing applied policy work. These exercises in logical-deductive theory become the final products and much of what goes under the name "applied economics" is actually simply a logical deductive exercise recasting a general theory for a particular case.

In Marshall's time, the general sensibility of economics could be conveyed to students relatively simply; empirical methods had yet to be developed to the level where one could reasonably think of formally testing a model, and the generally accepted models were not beyond the analytic capabilities of the students.

By the 1960s when Friedman's influence was at its peak, that was changing, and in the 1990s it has changed enormously. Today, it is essentially impossible for the majority of students to learn both the sensibility and institutional knowledge necessary to conduct the art of economics effectively, and the techniques necessary to conduct research in the positive science of economics. If they learn about history and institutions, they don't have time to learn how to conduct research at the highest level of theory; similarly if they learn the appropriate techniques for extending the theory, they don't have time to learn about the institutional and political sensibilities necessary to apply a theory. Division of labor is necessary—and the appropriate training of applied-policy economists significantly differs from the training of economic scientists concerned about extending the model.

CONCLUSION

I began the chapter with the statement that Milton Friedman is a brilliant economist but that the majority assessment is that his work was ideologically flawed, and that the Marshallian economics he advocated has been superseded by

Walrasian economics. These criticisms, I believe, stand, if Friedman is viewed as a positive scientist as the profession currently defines positive economics—as logical-deductive exercises and empirical testing of those deductive results (testing which, as Rosenberg (1992) argues, seldom comes). But that, I argue, is not how he should be viewed; he should, instead, be viewed as an economic artist—as an applied policy economist extraordinaire. As an economic artist, Friedman has almost no peer in economics, and his primary artistic flaw has been his failure to make clear the importance of the artistic component of his economic science.

NOTES

*   I would like to thank Daniel Hamond, Thomas Mayer, Abe Hirsch, and Kevin Hoover for comments on early drafts of this chapter.
1.   To say that Friedman's approach is not mainstream is not to say that Friedman stands alone; he has widespread support and respect in the mainstream profession as a "grand old man"—as a pioneer who, like many pioneers, has been outrun by methodological and technical advances.
2.   J.N. Keynes saw the scope of positive economic inquiry as applying only to economics, but it need not be so limited. For example, one could be advocating a positive social science and be searching for generalized rules of human action.
3.   The only one of these that directly negates my rules for the art of economics is #1. I discuss that difference in an appendix.

APPENDIX: FRIEDMAN AND INSIDE AND OUTSIDE VIEWS OF BEHAVIOR

The one methodological rule that Hirsch and De Marchi (1990) attribute to Friedman that does not fit my list of rules for the art of economics discussed in the text is the rule: "Adopt an 'outside' view of behavior." Hirsch and De Marchi interpret this rule as denying the ability to build realistic models and denying the applicability of introspection in considering issues (p. 162).

As I understand it, Hirsch and De Marchi are suggesting that Friedman uses an anti-general theory rule—a rule which would deny the existence of any positive economics as I define it, leaving only art. Hirsch and De Marchi recognize that this is a likely interpretation and specifically argue that this is the wrong interpretation. They suggest that the rule leaves a role for theory "as a creative process, introducing potentially useful interjections between broad sets of ideas and the data and the problems at hand" (p. 155). This is reminiscent of Marshall's "engine of analysis" interpretation of the role of theory. But in Marshall there is a definite role for introspection. As Hammond (1991b) points out, Marshall maintained one fundamental idea—the driving force to equilibrium of supply and demand—in considering issues. Marshall did not require the observer to take an outside view of behavior and used educated introspection throughout his analysis. Thus, "the outside view of behavior" rule is not consistent with Marshall's engine of analysis use of theory; it is an enormously strong rule which limits the use of certain types of common sense when approaching problems.

Moreover, it is unclear to me how anyone can achieve an outside view of behavior. Friedman certainly did not. Consider Friedman's statement about the role of the market in his *Price Theory: A Provisional Text* (1961). He writes:

> In any short period of time when the amount of a product is relatively fixed, there must be some way of adjusting consumption to production. This rationing must be accomplished in one way or another. There may be rationing by favoritism, bribery, chance, or by prices. When people are allowed to bid freely for goods, even if the quantity of the goods available is completely fixed, prices will adjust themselves in such a fashion that the quantity people want to buy *at the market price* is equal to the quantity available. Prices, therefore, do three things in solving the above five problems. They transmit information effectively and efficiently; they provide an incentive to users of resources to be guided by this information; and they provide an incentive to owners of resources to follow this information. (p. 10)

This, he claims, is a descriptive statement, not a justification of markets. He continues:

> In any normative judgment of the price system on the basis of the preceding description, several things must be kept in mind. First, this description implicitly supposes the existence of effective competition in translating consumer wishes into productive activity. It is assumed that people can affect their incomes only through use of their resources and not through interference with the price system. There is freedom to compete but not freedom to combine. Second, the controlling force is pecuniary demand; voting is in proportion to the number of dollars a person has. This is not obviously "just." The basic inequality, it should be noted, is an inequality in the ownership of resources. What the market does is primarily to determine the return per unit of resource, and there is no reason to believe that the market aggravates the inequality of the ownership of resources. Moreover, any given degree of inequality is a much more serious one in an economy which is governed largely by status or tradition than in a market economy where there is much chance for shifts in the ownership of resources. Historically, the fundamental inequality of economic status has been and is almost certainly greater in economies that do not rely on the free market than in those that do. (p. 11)

The first part of the above statement is his summary of the information of positive economic theory. It does not prove that the prices that actual markets reach transmit information effectively and efficiently. If it is description, as he states it is, it is description that is based on his introspection. This is not surprising since description necessarily involves interpretation of observations and those interpretations are necessarily influenced by one's sense, which is acquired from introspection. A complete outside view of human behavior is impossible.

Friedman is tentatively willing to take the above insight from economic theory as true. He is further willing to make the provisional judgment that further theorizing about the market has little to add to this important insight, so he moves on to applied policy issues. Many economists do not accept that judgment; work in what is called the positive branch of economics is designed to get a better handle on how prices transmit information effectively and efficiently.

The second part of the statement involves his subjective judgments about how politics, economics, and sociology interact. These judgments may be reasonable, but they are not derived from economic theory; they are derived from introspection—from a sense of the way the real world works, or what Hirsch and De Marchi (1990) call an "insider" view of behavior. If that is correct, then, in making these judgments, it seems that in this general statement about doing economics Friedman has violated the methodological prescription Hirsch and De Marchi attribute to him.

My conclusion from the above discussion is that the outsider rule that Hirsch and De Marchi attribute to Friedman is not quite descriptive of Friedman's methodology. His methodology is slightly more complicated. He is quite willing to accept the theoretical insights given in the page 10 quotation cited above. He is also willing to make certain judgments about political, social, and institutional realities based on introspection. These judgments, combined with the insight of economic theory, lead to the conclusion that prices transmit information effectively and efficiently, and they do it better than any other means of rationing. With this conclusion, why do any further work on abstract economic theory? Only the applied policy branch of economics remains relevant. And, given his judgments about politics and institutions, the applied policy goal of economics should be to convey that theory of how the market works to lay people who are not privy to that deep insight about the market.

Thus I would disagree with Hirsch and De Marchi that Friedman's methodological thinking can be characterized as adopting an outside view of behavior; instead, I would argue it involves adopting one big inside view of behavior—that markets work—and thereafter, an outside view.

Many economists were not willing to take that one big inside view of behavior—and, hence, could not follow Friedman's economic methodology. The alternative for them was presented as the logical deductive Walrasian approach. The choice they faced was (1) follow a Walrasian approach and question the effectiveness and efficiency of markets; or (2) follow a Marshallian/Friedman approach and do not question the effectiveness and efficiency of the market. Relying on an underlying positivist, scientific philosophy, most economists chose the Walrasian approach because it seemed the most honest scientific approach, the one most consistent with their interpretation of the theoretical work on markets—that given specific assumptions the market was efficient and effective, but given other assumptions, it might not be. This view allowed a role for positive logical-deductive economics considering when markets were efficient and when not.

Essentially, in this chapter the approach I am proposing for most economists is a third approach: Follow a Friedman policy-oriented method approach, but leave open the possibility of questioning the effectiveness and efficiency of the market. Doing so requires one to take an inside view of behavior, admitting that economic theory does not tell us that real-world markets necessarily transmit information effectively and efficiently, but otherwise is quite consistent with Friedman's methodological approach.

PART II

Methodology of the Art of Economics

3. The Art of Economics by the Numbers*

Most textbooks divide economics into two categories: positive and normative economics. They then go on to discuss the methodology of positive economics, focusing on broad rules that can be reduced to variants of the following: Develop a formal model; derive an hypothesis and empirically test that hypothesis with technical econometrics. These broad rules may or may not be appropriate for the building and testing of general theories, laws, or insights that are meant to become the structural basis for economic thinking; they are not appropriate for what most economists do, which is applied policy economics. Applied policy economics is a third branch of economics, a branch that builds down—that relates the abstract insights of economic models to real-world problems.

Exactly where applied policy economics fits into the positive/normative criteria is subject to some confusion. Many economists today, following Friedman, see it as part of the positive branch of economics. Others see it as belonging in welfare economics and hence as part of the normative branch of economics. This confusion about where to place it is understandable, since it belongs in neither positive nor normative economics. It belongs in a third category that J.N. Keynes, to whom Friedman credits the positive/normative distinction, called the art of economics.[1] According to Keynes, the art of economics was that branch of economics that relates the insights learned in positive economics to the goals determined in normative economics.

In making this positive/art distinction it is not necessary to place art in juxtaposition to science. Both positive economics and the art of economics can fall under the broad rubric of economic science. Regardless of whether it is necessary, Keynes' use of the term "art" to describe one of the three branches of economics has bothered many economists who are sympathetic to the need to do applied policy work. They see calling applied policy work "art" and the development of theories "positive" economics as demeaning to applied policy work. I don't see the term "art" as demeaning, nor do I see "science" as a higher level of activity than art. I would be delighted were people to think of me as an economic artist. However, given the normal economist's reaction to the term "art," it may have been better to have called this branch the "engineering branch" of economic science.

WHY DISTINGUISH THREE BRANCHES OF ECONOMICS?

There are a number of reasons for distinguishing among three branches of economics rather than between two. The most important reason is that different methodological rules apply to each. In building up a theory, or general law, about how the economy works, the task is to generalize from specifics—to abstract from the specifics of one's knowledge and develop models that elegantly capture relationships that transcend any specific instance. In the pursuit of general rules, Friedman's F-twist is relevant. The more elegant the theory, the more removed from real-world assumptions the theory is.

An example of a successful generalization is the general constrained maximization model of choice. Once learned, that model captures many of the specific insights of production and choice theory. Another would be the rules of optimal taxation, such as the Ramsey rule, which elegantly captures specific insights about efficiency and taxation. An even more elegant model is general equilibrium theory, which captures insights into the aggregate economy.

There is an empirical aspect to this search for general theories; somehow one must determine when a generalization, law, or theory is to be accepted as tentatively true and when a generalization is to be rejected. Most discussion in the philosophy of science and in the methodology of economics has focused on rules relevant to generalizing, formalizing, and accepting or rejecting these generalizations or theories.

In this methodological discussion of positive economics it is generally accepted that economists are trying to understand the economy for the sake of understanding; they are designing abstract models and formal tests of those models to determine whether they are "true," or at least not yet falsified.

The reason the methodological rules in the art of economics are different is that in applied policy economics one's objective is fundamentally different. In the art of economics one accepts the general laws and models that have been determined by the profession and one tries to apply the insights of economic models to real-world problems. Applied policy economics has nothing to do with testing a theory; it has to do with applying the insights of that theory to a specific case.

In applied policy economics Friedman's F-twist is quite inappropriate because one is trying to translate down from abstract theories to the real world. This means that one must take account of real-world institutions and frictions that were abstracted from in the development of the theory. There is an empirical element of applied policy economics, just as there is in the developing of the theory, but it involves a fundamentally different type of empirical work; it follows that the distinction between art—applied policy economics—and positive economics—developmental theory economics—is *not* based on an empirical/deductive theory distinction as some, especially Thomas Mayer (1993b), have suggested. The distinction is based on whether one is working toward developing theories, or toward *applying* theories that have already been developed.

A second reason for differentiating the art of economics from positive economics is to separate out the normative goals from the positive theory. This was the reason Keynes gave for separating them. Otherwise, one will have a tendency to give too much "scientific" weight to precepts which do not follow from theory but are, instead, based upon a combination of theory and institutional and political scientific judgments. Keynes writes that "unless the distinction between theorems and precepts is carefully borne in mind, the relativity of the former is likely to be overstated" (Keynes, p. 65). Terence Hutchison (1964), extending Keynes' reasoning, similarly argued for the importance of separating positive economic theory from normative economic thinking as much as possible.[2]

Let's consider an example: tariffs. Economic theory does not say whether or not tariffs are desirable for individual countries. There are numerous theoretical exceptions to their use, and qualifications to the proposition that tariffs reduce welfare. Tariffs can help individual countries at the expense of others. But, based on judgments about historical study of real-world cases, most economists are willing to ignore these qualifications and support free trade. But that support is based on historical and institutional judgment. It is not a theoretical law of positive economics; it is an applied policy precept. Often this distinction is not made because economists don't make the positive/art distinction.

An argument can be made that much of the formalist development of positive theory was done to offset the tendency of some economists to claim too much for the market. Examples of claiming too much for the market include J.B. Clark's well known argument that the market distribution of income was fair, the well known utilitarian arguments that the market maximized societal welfare, and the Chicago view that laissez faire was the appropriate policy that followed from economic theory. Formal theorists have shown that the logical reasoning for each of these arguments does not follow directly from economic theory without large numbers of provisos. For such conclusions to be drawn from theory, additional elements must be added to the analysis. These additional elements involve judgments on which reasonable people may differ and hence precepts—rules to guide policy—based on them belong in the art of economics and not in the positive branch of economics.

THE GROWING IMPORTANCE OF SEPARATING POSITIVE ECONOMICS FROM THE ART OF ECONOMICS

The need to distinguish applied policy work from positive work is an important one. Its importance has grown over time because of the increasingly technical sophistication of positive economic research which increases the importance of division of labor. Adam Smith's insight applies to economics as well as to pins.

In the early stages of a discipline, as theory and initial insights in a field are developing, a formal separation of an applied policy branch from a positive developmental theory branch is far less important, and probably impossible: general theories develop from specific applications as one tries to separate out the generalities from the specifics. But, over time, as more areas are looked into, agreement on more generalities becomes widespread, and these general insights are codified into elegant formal models. This happened to neoclassical micro economics in the 1930s, '40s, and '50s, as economists such as Abba Lerner, John Hicks, and Paul Samuelson codified the static individual maximization model into what has become the core of economic theory.

Once this codification occurs, combining applied policy and positive theoretical work no longer makes sense, since doing so does not take full advantage of the codification. One of the primary reasons for codifying insights is to be able to convey them more efficiently to others, including those doing applied policy work. Once one knows the generalized maximization principle, one knows the way it will work out in a variety of general settings. To take advantage of the codification, individuals doing applied policy work should not technically work out the implications of the maximization principle in each individual case. It is wasteful and inefficient to redevelop the wheel in each specific case to which the theory is being applied. One only need adapt the generally-known result to the specifics of the case being considered.

It follows that the development of a codified theory requires a significant change in how applied policy economics is conducted. *After codification, the further development of theory and applied policy work must be separated and that separation increases as theory is more developed.* One group of researchers—those in the positive branch—need to become more abstract and technical, further developing, extending, and testing the theoretical dimensions of the model. A second group of researchers—the applied policy branch—needs to become less technical and more institutionally oriented, as they determine how the insights of the codified theory can be applied in specific instances where the particulars of the case don't fit the assumptions of the theory.

Each of these branches involves both a theoretical component and an empirical component, but the structure and rules used in these components will differ between the two branches. For example, formally modifying the generalized model to particular cases may be a useful exercise for students to teach them the generalized model, but it is not a good way to conduct applied policy economics. Similarly, once a generalized model is developed, it makes little sense to test specific implications of that generalized model, other than as an educational exercise. If one believes the generalized model, one believes it applies; applied policy economics has nothing to do with empirically testing theories; it has to do with applying theories—theories that one is willing to tentatively accept as true—to the real world. To do that, one must add back into the model all the assumptions that were made as it was being generalized. The question in applied policy economics concerns whether the theory fits the application, not whether the theory is true. The applied policy issue is: How can the insights of positive economic theory be translated into real-world policies which achieve society's goals, taking account of real-world institutions, as well as the sociological and political dimensions of the policy?

PREVIOUS WORK ON THE METHODOLOGY FOR THE ART OF ECONOMICS

Keynes, who developed the three-part division of economics, provided little guidance to researchers as to how to do applied policy economics. His discussion of methodology of the art of economics was almost Feyerabendish—almost anything goes. He simply said that it would be loose and would include many non-economic factors. He did not try to provide any methodological benchmarks by which to judge applied policy work.

This lack of discussion about the methodology appropriate for the art of economics is unfortunate. The mere fact that methodological prescriptions for the art of economics must deal with integrating abstract theory with real-world observations and hence must include many non-economic factors does not mean that anything goes. On the contrary, when work is loose and includes non-economic factors, there is more need for methodological prescriptions.

Later economists also have had little to say about methodological prescriptions for applied policy work, at least in the literature with which I am familiar. One exception is Andrew Kamarck, whose excellent book, *Economics and the Real World,* makes a number of the same points that I make in this chapter.

A second exception is Thomas Mayer's *Truth versus Precision in Economics,* whose methodological discussion parallels mine in many ways. The difference is that Mayer specifically does *not* distinguish the methodology

appropriate for applied policy economics from the methodology appropriate
for positive economics. Instead, he discusses the methodology for what he
calls "empirical science economics."[3]

My approach differs from Mayer's in advocating a distinct split between
the methodology and teaching of positive economics—how to develop and
test theories—and the methodology and teaching the art of economics—applying theories to the real world to policy issues.[4] I am making no claims
about how positive economics should be undertaken. Whereas Mayer laments
positive theory becoming more abstract and technical, I see such abstract work
as necessary to refine theoretical insights. Somehow Mayer, like Friedman, of
whose work Mayer's is a continuation, sees the insights of economic theory
as simply existing, rather than being developed by a separate branch of economics—the branch that I call positive economics.

The difference between Mayer's and my approaches can be seen in our
evaluation of what he calls "fingertip economics," which he defines as "a less
formal, more intuitive theory that can be applied to every nook and cranny of
economic life" (p. 16). His book calls for a return to fingertip economics—
which most people will remember as the old Chicago approach. I do not. In
my view much of fingertip economics was the equivalent to the playing of
Chopsticks on the piano. It is wonderful as an exercise for teaching students
economic theory, but it is not a good way to conduct applied policy analysis.
Because it fails to distinguish art from positive economics, the Chicago approach tends to confuse economic precepts and economic laws, and to make
it seem as if the economic theory leads to policy conclusions without the
addition of the researcher's judgment. A second reason I oppose fingertip
economics is that much of it is too formal for applied policy work and not
formal enough for good positive economic work.

Much of fingertip economics is simply modifying the general model to
particular cases. Because it is generally done in a semi-formal maximizing
model, it requires the researcher to abstract from real-world institutions and
explain everything within a pure economic framework, rather than to integrate non-quantifiable, non-economic factors into the analysis. The type of
semi-formal theory and semi-formal empirical work fingertip economics involved led to enormous confusion, and to a tendency to use methodology
appropriate for building up theory when doing applied policy work. Thus
whereas my approach calls for two increasingly polar branches of economics:
a positive branch—a highly abstract, deductive, branch in which work is subject to rigorous empirical tests before it allows an insight to become a law, and
an art branch: a loose, non-formal, application of the theoretical insights to
the real world, Mayer's approach calls for a single semi-formal methodology
and no separation of art/positive branches.

Despite this difference, one will notice a distinct similarity between the methodological rules I will list for the art of economics and those that could be gleaned from Mayer's book. Given the overwhelming dominance of formalism in the modern economics profession, we are far more in agreement than we are in disagreement.

METHODOLOGICAL RULES FOR THE ART OF ECONOMICS

I will now proceed to list and discuss some methodological rules for the art of economics that I believe would be useful ones for applied policy economists to follow. The methodological rules are not meant to be binding constraints, but are instead meant as rough guides to approaching issues of applied policy. I fully recognize that every case is different and believe that if a good reason (consistent with the sense, if not the letter, of these rules) exists for breaking a rule, then it should be broken. But a methodological rule should be broken by explicit intent, not out of lack of consideration.

Rule #1: Do Not Violate the Law of Significant Digits.

I list this rule first because it is the one I believe is most often violated. Failure to follow this law of significant digits does not make the research wrong, it simply makes the research far less relevant than it otherwise would be. Let me give an example of violating the law of significant digits. Say you are multiplying these numbers:

$$2.04271 \times 4.0446 \times y \text{ where } 3 < y < 4.$$

What is the appropriate way to carry out the multiplication? One could fully multiply out the first two numbers and then multiply the result by 3 and 4 and use some averaging procedure. The answer arrived at by that process is not logically wrong; the process is, however, inefficient, and in violation of the law of significant digits. It involves much wasted work with no gain in accuracy. Thus, it would be inappropriate methodology according to the law of significant digits. Instead, one would more reasonably round off to, say, the nearest 10th and get an approximate answer between 24 and 32. Any more precise result presents false accuracy and would likely be misleading. A result can be no more accurate than the least significant digit.[5]

Much of what goes under the name of applied economic policy work violates this law all the time. Inevitably one needs to create a proxy which is only a loose representation of the variable one is interested in. Alternatively, there are qualitative variables that cannot be precisely measured but which must be integrated into the analysis to come to a policy conclusion. That is the nature of applied policy economics.

The current standard practice of most academic applied economists is to create a precise model, to calculate precise results, and then to add vague qualifiers. Doing so is just as wrong as carrying on the above multiplication to 10 decimal points.

The law of significant digits also applies to empirical work. If adding back the real-world assumptions is an imprecise process, then there is no advantage to precise empirical work. Applied policy statistical work should be far less precise than developmental theory statistical work, which is not applying accepted theory, but is determining whether accepted theory should be changed.[6]

Rule #2: Be Objective; Use the Reasonable Person Criterion to Judge Policy.

The normative goals of society are many, and policies are ultimately made to achieve society's normative goals. Good applied policy work explains how the real-world goals of society are advanced by a policy.

Positive economic methodology that focuses on a formal model is not especially helpful to meeting this criterion. The problem is that the generalized maximization model sheds little light on the multidimensional, and possibly lexicographic, goals of society. That formal model leads researchers to focus on efficiency in the formal model, treating distributional, moral, and institutional issues as addenda. Doing so is inappropriate for applied policy work. All considerations that could lead the model to differ from a researcher's sense of the appropriate concerns of society should be given equal marginal consideration.

Unlike the situation in positive economics where, potentially (although in practice they seldom do), the formal empirical tests determine whether one accepts or rejects a theory, in the art of economics there is no escaping judgment. Society's goals are inevitably poorly specified, and they are often contradictory. Yet, to come to a conclusion about a real-world policy proposal, one must come to grips with these contradictory goals, and either help clarify them (which falls under the category of normative economics), or show how one's policy proposal will best meet the real-world contradictory goals. Focusing on Pareto-optimality as a goal, or on some abstractly specified social welfare function, as is generally done in much of what goes under the name, "welfare economics," is unacceptable for applied policy work since Pareto-optimality or abstractly-specified social welfare functions are not descriptions of real-world goals. Instead, one should use a reasonable person criterion:

would a representative reasonable person in society favor a policy proposal once he or she understood the implications and effects as well as the researcher does? Thus, questions like the following must be explicitly dealt with: What are the distributional consequences of the policy? What groups will be helped and what groups will be hurt, in both the short run and the long run? What senses of morality will the policy upset? Why should those senses be over-ruled? What effect will the policy have on existing institutions?

Applied policy work requires the researcher to make value judgments, but that does not mean the researcher should not maintain objectivity. The goals in relation to which a researcher discusses policies should be well specified. (They very likely will have been determined by others specializing in norma-tive economics.) Those goals might be quite different from the economist's own goals. Since the art of applied policy is so messy, and since one cannot rely on formalization to help keep one's values out of the analysis, the re-searcher must be even more careful than in positive economics to be open about his or her judgments about society's goals, the value of existing institu-tions, and the way in which government works to achieve those goals.

Rule #3: Use the Best Economic Theory Available.

Work in applied policy economics—in the art of economics—has a symbiotic relationship with work in positive theory. Work in positive economics should be constantly challenging assumptions of the currently accepted model, test-ing the models as best one can, and providing alternative formulations of existing theories and models. The work will often be highly technical and obscure. Most of it will have little relevance to applied policy economics, but some will, and the applied policy theorist will have to make judgments about the relevance of new theoretical developments.

An applied policy economist would stay familiar with advances in positive theory, but would be unlikely to take part in it. Where there are competing theories, he or she would know the competing theories, considering their policy proposals and analysis in relation to all competing theories.

One example of what I mean is the following: The standard theory of the labor markets suggests that wages and salaries follow certain laws; modern efficiency wage theories have called standard theories into question and an applied policy economist should be aware of the different implications of the new theory and, where needed, change his or her policy prescriptions to fit the "new common sense" that follows from the new theory.

A second example concerns recent developments in game theoretic foun-dations of general equilibrium that suggest that multiple aggregate equilibria will exist and that sunspot and bubble equilibria cannot be ruled out. These developments have profound implications for applied policy macroeconomics that the applied policy economist would have to deal with.

Rule #4: Take in All Dimensions of the Problem.

Formal work in positive economics is necessarily limited by the formal tools available. Thus, the model will not necessarily fit the problem; the problem will be constructed to fit the available techniques. In a sense it will be focused on parts of the chain of analysis that are the strongest, and develop those. In applied policy economics a formal model exists only as an aid to one's understanding. It isn't being tested.

Work in applied policy economics cannot take that approach. The problem being considered, not the techniques, must guide the analysis. If administrative costs are important to the policy and they aren't included in the formal model, they must be built into the analysis; if effects of the policy on institutions are important but are not considered in the theoretical model, then those must be taken into account. If some of those effects are only roughly quantifiable, then, following the law of significant digits, there is little sense in precisely quantifying other aspects of the analysis. Similarly, there is little gain in carrying out statistical tests of significance on a well-defined model.

Rule #5: Use Whatever Empirical Work Sheds Light on the Issue at Hand.

The role of empirical work in the art of economics is quite different from the role of empirical work in positive economics. In positive economics one is trying to test the validity of theories; in the art of economics one is trying to apply theories. Empirical work is giving one a feel for the data; data mining is quite acceptable, even encouraged, as a way of getting a handle on the intricate dynamic interrelationships that are beyond the formal theory. Vector autoregression and other measurement without theory techniques are acceptable.

This freedom to use data to get a feel for the problem comes at a cost, however. That cost is that the standard classical statistical tests that were designed to formally test theories are no longer valid. A researcher cannot rely on them to tell him or her whether his or her statistical work is meaningful; the researcher must rely on his or her judgment.

In the art of economics, often, a scatter plot of one variable against another is more useful than a formal econometric analysis. The need for informality in empirical work is reinforced by the fact that many of the relevant empirical facts will be non-quantifiable. When this is the case, the law of significant digits makes most precise empirical work a waste of time.

Rule #6: Do Not be Falsely Scientific; Present only Empirical Tests that Are Convincing to You.

Rule #5 does not mean that statistical tests should not be done; it does, however, mean that they are to be used as a guide to the researcher, not as a scientific test of the model of the effects of a policy. To present them as something other than they are is to be falsely scientific and that is a fundamental methodological error in the art of economics. Currently, as Mayer nicely discusses (pp. 132–151), economists violate this rule all the time. In fact, they violate it so much that all economists reading other economists' work can discount the scientific claims and reasonably correctly interpret the results. But as Mayer also discusses, there is a tendency not to do robustness tests, which would be required to make empirical work convincing. In the art of economics one would do, and report, whatever empirical work that is helpful to guide you to a policy conclusion.

THE INTERACTION OF WRITTEN AND UNWRITTEN METHODOLOGICAL RULES

For the majority of economists who are working in applied policy jobs directly subject to market forces, the above stated methodological rules are the ones they already follow. Their advancement depends on the relevance of their work; since the above rules are designed to see that applied policy work is relevant, the above rules relate closely to the institutional incentives they face. Thus, these rules are not directed at them. They are, instead, directed at academic economists. Even though the majority of these academic economists consider themselves applied policy economists and they are training students in applied policy economics, they find themselves subject to the methodological rules of developmental theory science in their unwritten rules even as they are teaching and doing research in applied policy economics. They face implicit directives to develop formal models and rigorously test these models and, since they are doing applied policy economics, to make those formal models relevant to policy. These are *impossible* directives, but if one's job depends on meeting directives, they are directives that will be superficially met with tests that look rigorous, but often aren't, and models that look impressive and formal but are in fact vacuous, or are simply reformulations of models that already exist. It is those academic economists that I am interested in affecting.

I don't expect to affect these academic economists directly. Almost the only people who read methodological discussions are other methodologists.

Put simply, most economists don't care about formal methodology; they are concerned with institutional requirements for advancement. So I am under no illusion that the above methodological rules will be considered by anybody other than methodologists.

But that does not mean that formal methodological discussions are irrelevant; far from it. Methodologists have much greater influence than they realize. But that influence is indirect, through the brief general discussion of methodology that filters into textbooks, and the influence that discussion has on tenure rules and editorial decisions. In that filtering process, the prescriptions and insights of methodological specialists likely will be perverted, but something will remain. That something has been Friedman's positive/normative distinction and the implicit acceptance that economists' work should be judged by the rules of formal positive science. Almost all methodological writings in economics have accepted that premise and have carried out the methodological discussion of positive economics to high levels, taking up the problems in defining science, in carrying out good science, and in choosing among competing theories. Much of that writing has been critical of what economists do, but because it has accepted the proposition that economists are supposed to do positive theoretical science, that writing has reaffirmed the positive/normative distinction and thereby reinforced, rather than challenged, the existing methodological practices.

If methodologists no longer reaffirm the positive/normative distinction, the textbooks will have to deal with the issue. If methodologists agree that applied policy economics should have a different set of methodological rules than does the positive science of economics, the textbooks will have to deal with the issue since there is a strong demand by students and society to have economists teach applied policy economics. As that happens, those rules will begin filtering down through textbooks to incoming students, and thereby make a difference in what they see as good economics. As it does so, it will have other impacts and eventually it will influence what really matters to academic economists: tenure criteria and editorial policy of journals.

The current positive methodological prescriptions have created unwritten rules for academic economists that go something like the following: Publish often in those journals that are highly ranked; don't worry about real-world applicability of the analysis; adopt a new technique; don't waste time discussing institutions; make sure you do some empirical test, the more formal the better, and see that you get reasonably good results; briefly mention policy implications at the end, but state that more work is needed. Variants of these rules are also conveyed to graduate and undergraduate students as they choose their research or dissertation topics: Choose a topic that's feasible; choose a topic for which you can develop a formal model; choose a topic for which there's some data with which you can empirically test the model, ideally using a new econometric technique that's just been developed; choose a topic that you can divide up into publishable papers relatively quickly.

In short, the combination of this push for publication and the background positive methodological rules leads academic researchers to do precisely what I argued makes little sense for applied policy work—to modify one assumption of an existing model at a time and to examine the result, while leaving out many assumptions that intuitively would fundamentally change the model's results when applied to reality.[7] If a journal can be found to publish it, the incentives are for a professor to publish such an article. If one can't be found, the incentives are for a group of professors to get together and start one.

One could argue that the existence and growth of applied journals of the type I am describing implies that there is a demand by society for their output. I find that argument unpersuasive. The demand for most applied economics journals is generated by university libraries which generally respond to requests of professors themselves. Publishers see academic journals as potential cash cows for which they can charge up to hundreds of dollars per subscription.[8] Even if only a few professors succeed in getting their libraries to buy that journal, it will generate enough income to be sustainable. Moreover, librarians have an inherent compulsion to acquire complete sets and, once started, they dislike breaking off a subscription. The result is that many, if not most, applied policy journals exist in large part to provide publication outlets for academic economists, not to influence policy. Since the process of supplying journal articles has value to the writer independent of the value of those articles to society, it pays faculty either to subsidize the demand for these journals themselves or to get their schools to subsidize demand, by having their library subscribe.

There are many journals of applied economics out there—and there are more everyday. But many of the articles in these journals are pedagogical exercises. They take the general maximizing model; modify it slightly, sometimes by simply redefining some terms; and show how the modified general maximizing model looks in this particular case. Such articles give little or no guidance to real world policy because they do not address the policy-relevant questions: Are the assumptions reasonable? Do the goals the model achieves match the normative goals one has decided upon? Is the suggested policy administratively feasible? The economist often has ideas about these issues, but the current methodological rules do not allow the author to discuss them; it wouldn't be good science. It would, however, be good applied policy work. The reality is that issues relevant for policy seldom have a general answer. The reality is that most of these applied policy issues cannot usefully be considered in relation to technical models. The reality is that applied policy issues inevitably must be done by someone with an intricate knowledge of real-world institutions.

Many academic economists I've talked with agree that much of what is currently called applied policy work is actually simply a ticket to tenure. Researchers who believe that, but do currently acceptable applied policy work anyhow, justify what they are doing with the argument that everyone is doing it; if they didn't, they would not get tenure and they would be out of a job. And they are right. The unwritten methodological rules state that if a journal will accept an article modifying the wheel for the nth time, it is an article worth writing.

CONCLUSION

I believe the above description of what happens when positive economic methodology is used in applied economics is understood by most economists. Nonetheless, most economists would prefer to ignore it, either because they are caught up in the tenure/publication process or find that their training has not prepared them to do good applied policy work. Given individual incentives, I can understand that position. But methodological prescriptions are not designed to make people's lives easy, or to get them tenure; they are designed to make compatible the goals of what the discipline is trying to achieve with what individuals are trying to achieve, given existing institutional incentives.

Where the institutional framework creates perverse incentives, strong methodological rules must exist to counter the perverse incentives. These rules, however, are not for young economists; they are for the economists who determine the institutional rules; they are for reviewers of journals; they are for tenure committees; they are for dissertation advisors; they are for outside reviewers of academic programs. These are the groups who determine institutional incentives. If these groups judge young economists by the methodological guidelines of the art of economics rather than by the guidelines of positive economics, then applied policy work will become more relevant.

NOTES

*   I would like to thank Kevin Hoover, Abe Hirsch, Thomas Mayer, and Roger Backhouse for helpful comments on earlier drafts of this chapter.
1.   The term "art of economics" was not new with Keynes. It was much discussed in the literature in juxtaposition to science. Keynes' contribution was in focusing on a tripartite division, establishing art as a buffer between positive economics and normative judgments.
2.   Hutchison uses the term positive in a different way. In Hutchison's usage it includes much of what I classify as art, whereas his art includes much of what I include in normative economics. In my view, however, the differences between Hutchison and me are primarily terminological; our substantive approaches to economic methodology are similar.

3. In a separate paper (Mayer, 1993a), he makes clear that he sees his methodological approach as a continuation of Friedman's methodological approach.
4. The issue isn't whether different people do the work. I have no objection to the same people sometimes doing applied policy and sometimes doing developmental theory, but I argue that, if they do, they should use fundamentally different methodologies in each; Mayer seems to be arguing that only one methodology should be used in economics.
5. The theory of significant digits can itself become complicated, and precisely where one should round off can be a matter of debate. But the law is subject to itself, and in applied policy work, precisely where one rounds off is less important than that one does not grossly violate the law.
6. Mayer discusses a similar rule, which he calls the "strongest link" rule, citing Kamarck's and my discussion of the law of significant digits. It is reasonable to apply this law to all aspects of economics, but I argue that in applied policy work one must add back dimensions of the problem that are highly imprecise. Hence, in applied policy work, the law is a much stronger argument against the use of precise, formal models. In developmental theory, one can separate out parts of the chain that consist solely of stronger links, and hence one can achieve more rigor and precision.
7. Salim Fahid told me a wonderful story in which one economist tells another that an idea can be demonstrated 42 different ways and the other responds, "Great! That's 42 articles we can get out of it."
8. One well-known applied economic policy journal costs a library $775 per year.

4.   The Art of Monetary Policy*

Policy works because it has artists pulling the strings. This chapter is dedicated to one of those true artists, Alan Holmes. Holmes had a thirty-five-year career in public service, culminating in his position as the head of the Federal Reserve operations in both the domestic securities market and the foreign exchange markets. He was a genius at achieving policy consensus among disparate groups within the policy setting, making him both a formulator and an implementer of monetary policy. He understood both the highest level of theory and the most minute operational detail. The need for both policymakers and academic economists who write about policy to have this dual understanding is the central theme of this book.

It is a theme that is nicely illustrated by a story told by one of Holmes' colleagues, Paul Volcker. There was a squirrel in the forest who had a particular taste for fish. The squirrel went to the wise old owl for some guidance and counsel. After listening to his story, the owl advised the squirrel that the way for him to satisfy that desire was to become a kingfisher. So the squirrel happily went away, ran up a tree over a brook, and imagined himself a kingfisher so he could catch some fish. Of course, imagination was not enough. The squirrel discovered he was still a squirrel. After sitting in the tree for a while, he returned to the owl in a state of some agitation and railed, "You told me the way to satisfy my desire to get some fish was to become a kingfisher, but you haven't told me how to do that. I am still a squirrel." The owl replied, "Look, you came to me with a problem. I gave you some sound policy advice. The rest is operational detail."

We begin with this story because it captures the essential message of the book. *Understanding monetary policy requires an understanding of the operational details of monetary policy.* By operational details we mean more than just the technical means by which monetary policy is implemented; we mean the institutions and context within which policymakers approach an issue (for example, the existence of informal understandings and sensibilities that affect decisions) and the nuances of seemingly identical actions (the Fed buying Treasuries at 11:30 a.m. may mean something quite different than buying Treasuries at 1:00 p.m.).

It is necessary to know these operational details in order to do meaningful empirical work on monetary theory, to interpret data, and to choose between competing theories. If one does not know operational details yet is studying monetary theory or policy, one is playing irrelevant mind-games that may get one published, or through an exam, but that will have about as much meaning for the economy as the advice of the wise old owl had for the squirrel.

When Volcker told the story quoted above, he was picking on monetarists' single-minded focus on the money supply. The story, however, has broader relevance, and is directly applicable to many modern-day New Classical and New Keynesian monetary theorists, who, even more so than their predecessors, the monetarists and the various sorts of Keynesians, have lost sight of real-world institutions. Modern monetary theorists have become more and more deeply immersed in complicated theoretical constructs. The problem is that, complicated as these constructs are, they are nowhere near complicated enough; they lose many of the interactions and nuances that characterize the real-world institutions their theories purport to describe. This means that the subtleties of policy differences far exceed the subtleties of even the most complicated theories that can be taught to students. It follows that before such theories can be applied to the real world, these nuances and interactions must be included in the analysis. To do that in a meaningful way, one must have a deep sense of the institutions within which monetary policy is conducted.

Why do we belabor the obvious? Because much of the teaching of modern monetary theory and policy, both at graduate and undergraduate levels, has lost sight of the obvious. It is the teaching of theories and models—New Classical, New Keynesian, monetarist, global monetarist, neo-Keynesian, new-neo-Keynesian; there are many—without a meaningful operational context.

Instead of being taught that theories must be interpreted through a lens that reflects operational detail, students are taught to think through policy solely in relation to these models. They finish their courses with a knowledge of these models and the different strategies these models suggest for policy— you should use money supply as an intermediate target; you should use interest rates as an intermediate target; you should use a monetary rule; you should use discretion—and a belief that they can apply those models and the policies they studied to the real world.

That belief is an illusion. Few of the answers to specific questions about monetary policy depend on theoretical differences independent of institutional context. Most good policymakers can be monetarists one moment, Keynesians the next, and sometimes both simultaneously. They make decisions based on a sensibility and a feeling they have for the situation. That feeling and that sensibility are often related to their understanding of theories, but not in a straightforward way, at least not if they are good policymakers.

Let us give an example. One of the seminal ideas in New Classical economics was Finn Kydland and Edward Prescott's (1977) differentiation between a consistent and an optimal policy. An optimal policy is a policy that

The Lost Art of Economics

maximizes a social welfare function from a given point of time into the indefinite future. A consistent policy maximizes this same function, but is invariant over time. They showed that the consistent policy is preferable to the optimal policy.

The key insight that led them to their conclusion is that feedback effects of expected policy decisions can be important to current decisions; if future policy options are not restricted, individuals' current decisions will force policymakers to arrive at certain optimal, but, from a broader perspective, unreasonable, decisions. A good example is a child who wants ice cream and will scream incessantly if he or she does not get it. Let us say that the optimal policy is to give in. That might not be a reasonable policy. The consistent policy is to establish a rule from which it is impossible to deviate: No ice cream unless you eat your vegetables. Knowing that his or her parents cannot deviate from that rule, any rational child (and many real-world children) will modify his or her behavior, since the unmodified behavior will not produce ice cream and will make everyone worse off. The rule gets parents what they want and it involves less screaming, but this rule can only be implemented by limiting parents' discretion: they cannot give in, because they have made it impossible to do so.

This insight led Kydland and Prescott to a discussion of rules versus discretion in policymaking. In that discussion they equated rules with consistent policy, discretion with optimal policy, and proved that rules are preferred to discretion. They conclude:

> The implication of this analysis is that active stabilization may well be dangerous and it is best that it not be attempted. Reliance on policies such as a constant growth in the money supply and constant tax rates constitutes a safer course of action . . . policy makers should follow rules rather than discretion. . . . One possible institutional arrangement is for Congress to legislate monetary and fiscal policy rules and [for] these rules to become effective only after a 2-year delay. (Kydland and Prescott 1977, p. 476)

Kydland and Prescott's paper was seen to be, and was in fact, an important development in the academic debate about monetary policy. New Classical economics, of which the Kydland and Prescott paper was one part, was a useful response to many neo-Keynesian models in which everything looked clear cut. Neo-Keynesians had used comparative static models to draw implications about what the appropriate monetary policy should be—interest rate control versus money supply targeting, for example. Kydland and Prescott's paper was useful in showing that any comparative static model will be insufficient to answer such questions, that the way in which individuals form expectations, and how those expectations interrelate with policy, makes a difference in answering such questions. Like the game of scissors/rock/paper, these

New Classical models covered neo-Keynesian models, which themselves had covered earlier monetarist black box models.

But all of these academic mind-games are quite irrelevant to the debates about the conduct of monetary policy. Kydland and Prescott's proof of the superiority of rules over discretion is based on an assumption that one can have fully specified contingent rules. Unfortunately, because the future is unknown, the assumption cannot be met in the real world. Even coming close to meeting it—designing a contingency rule for all currently conceivable contingencies—is too costly to implement. Any real-world rule must be of limited contingency. For some contingencies you will want a rule; for others you will not. There is no general proof about the superiority of limited rules versus discretion. There is no escaping the need for situation-dependent judgment.

If one looks at the conduct of real-world monetary policy, it is clear that monetary policy has always been conducted with a distinction between optimal and consistent policy and with a deep understanding of dynamic feedback effects, just as most parenting is conducted with that same deep understanding. All policymakers, even parents with ice-cream-hungry kids, attempt to have rules. But every policymaker, and every economic agent, recognizes that rules can be broken depending on the situation.

The art of parenting is to impose your rules in a way that does not lead your child to total rebellion, while at the same time instilling in your child those values you want to instill (and to do it with children who also know the value of the "Cry until you get ice cream" rule, which seems to be instinctually conveyed at birth). The art of monetary policy is in finding the appropriate rule of limited contingency and in distinguishing those situations in which a rule can usefully be broken because the situation is a sufficiently unique historical event, or one with such long-run consequences that there will be no long run unless the rules are broken—from those situations that can be dealt with by rules. For example: Should the Fed bail out large banks? If it does, or can be expected to do so, the large bank will build that into its expectations, making it more necessary to bail out large banks, If the Fed does not bail out the large bank, the entire financial system may collapse. Alternatively, should a parent relent and give ice cream to a child who is dying from cancer? These are extreme examples, but deciding which case is typical and which case is not is a judgment call; no theory can lead to an answer.

THE SCRIBBLINGS OF REAL-WORLD PRACTITIONERS

We put together our volume, *The Art of Monetary Policy* (1994), because of our concern about the separation between theory and real-world policy. The essays in it are not the scribblings of academics; they are the scribblings of real-world practitioners—the artists of monetary policy. By bringing together essays by some of the most talented artists in the field, we hoped to begin to build bridges between theory and practice; we hoped to help students, who will become the future theorists and policymakers, get a better sense of the institutions and operations that are so fundamental for an understanding of monetary policy. We hoped to give them an entree into the art of monetary policy.

Using one's knowledge of theory combined with one's knowledge of the relationships and institutions to make reasonable decisions about monetary policy is what we mean by the art of monetary policy. You cannot get that operational knowledge from studying models or theory no matter what the flavor; you get it from studying institutions and their development. You get it from apprenticing yourself to those public servants who know the institutions, and to those people who have thought about them and immersed themselves in understanding them. Clearly, this is not the content of most economics students' training whether it be at the graduate or the undergraduate level. And that is a major flaw in economics students' training.

To tie one's hands in the hope of taking advantage of rules over discretion is also to tie one's hands in cases where discretion is called for. Kydland and Prescott's seminal work lagged far behind real-world decision making; with that work, academic economists' modeling techniques simply narrowed the lag between academic theoreticians and practitioners.

THE CONSEQUENCES OF TEACHING THEORY WITHOUT ART

The current practice of teaching students theory without art hurts both theory and policy. Theory is hurt in one way—it becomes theory for the sake of theory, theory unconnected to reality; policy is hurt in two ways—many potentially superb policymakers do not go into policy and the policy that is conducted does not have the benefit of informed theory. Let us first consider how theory is hurt.

HOW THEORY IS HURT BY CURRENT PRACTICES

Many graduate students in monetary economics go on to distinguished academic careers proving lemmas and theorizing about issues such as whether rules are better than discretion, whether monetary aggregates are preferable to interest rates as intermediate targets, how to add an equation to a model to make the model come up with a different answer, or how to test empirically whether this model or that model is preferable. This work is far less meaningful than it could be because many of these theorizers have no training in the art of applying economic models to policy issues. They try to squeeze answers out of theory that cannot be squeezed out. Theory without a deep sense of the institutions does not answer policy questions.

We are not arguing against theory or theorizing. Once people have information about the way the system actually works, they can generalize from it; they can simplify and condense their insights, and come up with relevant and useful models that embody their insights and knowledge. But those models do not have an existence independent of their creators' knowledge of the way the real world works. To judge whether a model is useful requires insights and institutional knowledge. A model is not a world unto itself; a model is simply a key that opens the door to the much more complicated and messy real world. Keynes summarized the issue nicely when he said, "Economics is a science of thinking in terms of models joined to the art of choosing models which are relevant to the real world."

Because of the nature of the model as a simplified representation of reality, it generally cannot be formally empirically tested in a meaningful way; the model is part and parcel of a larger vision. A model has meaning only with the large number of *ad hoc* assumptions and provisos in the back of the modeler's head that reflect that vision. If an empirical observation does not fit the model, the model will be adjusted to the vision. Understanding the vision behind the model is as important as understanding the model.

THE MONETARIST VISION AND THE KEYNESIAN VISION

Consider the monetarist and Keynesian visions. The monetarist vision is of a political climate in which government will too often give in to political pressures, will take the easy way out, and will consistently err on the side of using too much discretion. The Keynesian vision is of a political climate in which government will operate reasonably effectively even in the face of political pressures; while it might sometimes take the easy way out, it will generally conduct policy for the common good. The differences in monetarist and Keynesian policy proposals follow from the differences of those visions, not from any economic model. Yet the monetarist and Keynesian visions have seldom been discussed, and academics have forced the differences to show up in the shape of some curve or specification of a model.

What has happened is that Keynesian and monetarist models, freed from the institutional knowledge of their creators, acquired a life of their own. An equation was added here, a term reinterpreted there, and pretty soon one had a model with little or no relation to the vision. Moreover, as institutions changed, so too did the appropriate models to describe them. It would seem reasonable that sometimes the Keynesian vision fit reality and sometimes the monetarist vision fit reality. Given the changing problems and institutional structure, the two visions are not necessarily incompatible.

How many economics students are currently taught to view theories in this way? Few, we believe. Instead they are taught that one or the other theory must be right, and that the choice between the two must be made on the basis of formal empirical tests. When, instead of informal empirical tests of the larger vision, formal empirical tests are used to determine which model is preferable, the winning model becomes merely the result of a competition, with the winner determined by the ingenuity and perseverance of researchers in various groups. If you lose one round, you simply modify an *ad hoc* assumption and win the next until the debate fades away.

Has forty years of empirical testing determined whether the monetarist or the Keynesian model is the correct one? Does anyone believe that a definitive test exists? Instead of conclusively answering such questions, theorists simply pose new ones; thus the academic debate has shifted from a monetarist/Keynesian debate to a New Classical/New Keynesian debate. (The latest fad when we wrote this article was to look for unit roots in an attempt to test whether a data series generating function is, or is not, stationary. Unfortunately, as every artist knows, the future may be different from the past, so even if an answer is forthcoming based on past data, it will not definitively answer the policy question.)

ART AND THE COMPARATIVE ADVANTAGE OF EDUCATIONAL INSTITUTIONS

Many academics agree with us about the above arguments, but nonetheless argue that educational institutions should focus on models. They argue that universities have a comparative advantage in teaching science rather than art, theory rather than mundane operational details and insightful knowledge. How the world really works, they claim, is learned as much by osmosis as by teaching. They argue, "You don't teach artists by teaching them art theory; you teach them by having them practice, correcting them when they are wrong, showing them how to do it; and then, once they've learned how to do what can be done, you show them how to experiment and go beyond the current state of the art. The only way one learns the institutional sense necessary to judge models is to work in the institutions—to get a feel for those institutions and a sensibility about them—the university is not the place to get that."

We agree with the sensibility of such critics, but disagree with the conclusion. We believe that undergraduate and graduate schools can teach art, and that doing so would significantly improve economic education. True, art is best learned in real-world institutions, but that does not preclude it from being taught in the classroom.

Even if it is extraordinarily difficult to teach art, the conclusion—that because of academic economists' comparative advantage, they should teach only theory—does not follow. Such a conclusion would follow only if all graduate education in economics required a real-world apprenticeship in which all theorists gained first-hand knowledge of the real world. But that does not happen; no undergraduate or graduate economics program that we know of has such an apprenticeship program. Unless the art of economics is taught in graduate school, even taught badly, it will not be taught.

Unfortunately, the current situation is not only that the art of economics is not being taught. It is worse; graduate schools are not even teaching that it is important. Currently, students are given no sense of the limitations of what they are doing.

Thus, we believe that at a minimum, *it is still fundamentally important to teach students that the art of monetary policy is important, and that it is a necessary component of understanding the models, of testing models, and of working with the models.* The danger of not teaching the importance of the art of economics is that the students start seeing the model as the reality and they lose any interest in the reality that model is supposed to describe.

HOW POLICY IS HURT BY CURRENT PRACTICES

As we stated above, policy is hurt in two ways by current practices. The first way it is hurt has to do with the number of people planning to go on to work in policy. Many economists trained by academic institutions do, of course, go into policy jobs. The initial transition is difficult, but successful transfers quickly learn to forget most of what they learned in graduate school—to see it as a hurdle they had to get over to get to policy; not a necessary part of their training. And since one has to be bright to get over that hurdle, graduate schools serve as a screen for job applicants. In a good policy environment it takes about two months for a bright economist to learn that much of his or her graduate training is irrelevant to the real issues, and another two years or so to get a sense of the institutions and insights of current policymakers. So the system works, but it does not work as well as it could.

One reason the system does not work as well as it could is that many people who would make wonderful policymakers never go into policy at all. Schools operate like a filter and they are screening out large numbers of people. What happens is that potentially brilliant artists never become policymakers. Alan Holmes was a true artist; he had the integrity, the judgment, and a well-honed sense of how theory can be interpreted to be relevant to the real world. People like him make a system work. One of the most important jobs an educational system can fulfill is to train and prepare people like Holmes to go into public service. Our educational system is not fulfilling that role.

Let us give an example. Once, when Paul Volcker gave a speech at Yale, he asked some 350 or so students how many planned to go on into public service. The result: only one student said that he had such plans, and Volcker was not sure that student understood the question. Graduate schools in economics are no different. In interviews Klamer and Colander (1990) conducted with graduate students at top schools, many graduate students said they were talked out of going into policy work, even though the reason they had gone to graduate school in the first place was to prepare themselves for policy work. "Policy is for simpletons" is the view they heard from their teachers.

This does not mean that academics actually come out and say that policy is for simpletons (although some of the less discreet of them do say it), but it is the view that the students hear and absorb. By the end of three years of graduate economic education, most students are socialized into the academic way of thinking and are directed away from any policy work.

Again, Paul Volcker has a story that captures the problem. After leaving the Fed, he taught at Princeton. While there he was swamped with work and asked a junior colleague to assist him with a book he had agreed to do. The young colleague said no, that he could not work on a book on policy because it would ruin his career. Paul was surprised and later asked the departmental chairman if that were true. The departmental chairman thought for a moment and said, no, not if the young colleague did it only once.

The second way that policy is hurt by the current situation is that policy is robbed of the useful insights that would come from relevant and informed theorizing and modeling. Keynes once said that we are all slaves of some defunct economist, and by that he meant some defunct economic theorist. Policymaking is based on an implicit or explicit vision of how the economy works. Ultimately, theory lies behind that vision; theoretical advances help sharpen policymakers' vision. When theory is doing its job, theorists' work acts as a corrective lens on policymakers' visions, placing issues in different focus. Different theories provide a different focus on issues. Ultimately, policymaking requires an integration of the different visions that flow from different theories.

When theorists no longer relate their theories to visions, policymaking suffers. Currently, the vision taught to policymakers in their on-the-job training is the existing institutional vision. The students who come to work in policy are essentially *tabulae rasae*. They often have learned little in graduate school that cannot be quickly shown to be foolish or irrelevant. Because they have not developed their own judgment, after their on-the-job training is complete they are generally imprinted with the establishment vision. In the United States this means that a particular Fed vision is the one currently informally imprinted on incoming policymakers. The Fed vision may be right. But unless people trained in the art of policy outside the Fed interrelate with that vision, the Fed vision will tend to perpetuate itself, whether it be right or wrong. Currently, except within the Fed itself, there is little meaningful interaction of alternative visions that can lead to major policy changes and innovations.

NOTE

* This chapter was written jointly with Dewey Daane. It is adapted from our book, *The Art of Monetary Policy*.

PART III

Textbooks and the Art of Economics

5. Telling Better Stories in Introductory Macro

Teaching first-year economics involves telling stories. These stories are simplifications of far richer stories that we economists tell, test, and study. In first-year macro the stories we tell include multiplier stories, natural rate stories, and growth stories. We embody those stories in simple models, such as the AE/AP model, the AS/AD model, and a production-function-based growth model. These models structure our story and give professors something solid to hang exam questions on. Using the growth story we teach as a case in point, this chapter argues that structuring introductory macro stories around formal models makes the stories we tell unnecessarily boring to students.

WHY DOES ECONOMICS SEEM BORING WHEN IT ISN'T?

It is sometimes said that an economist is an accountant without a sense of humor. When introductory students hear that description, you can see them nodding in agreement; the reality is that most introductory students consider economics and the economists who teach it boring. We economists know that they are wrong; we are dynamic, exciting individuals, and the story we have to tell is fascinating, rich with all the ingredients of a great story: exciting story lines, plot, passion, and intrigue.

When I listen to top economists discuss their research, I'm infused with their passion and excitement. Unfortunately, something happens in the translation of that high-level story down to the first-year student: The exciting becomes the boring. An important reason why is the way in which we combine the telling of the story with the teaching of simple models.

THE PROBLEM WITH COMBINING INTRODUCTORY STORIES WITH FORMAL MODELS

The problem with tying our stories to formal models is that a large portion of our audience doesn't know the language of models, mathematics. Textbook authors and intro professors know that, and to make the models somewhat understandable to these students we water down the research models into "teaching models." Thus the stories we tell go through a multiple translation process—from a researcher's general understanding (1) to a research model, (2) to an easier intermediate pedagogical model, (3) to an even easier principles model, and finally (4) to a student's general understanding. At each stage of this multiple translation process some of the excitement of the economic story is lost. Our stories would be far less boring if we eliminated the multiple translation process and went directly from a researcher's general understanding to a student's general understanding.

It is only for the principles level that I am making this suggestion. I am fully aware that while we lose something whenever we translate ideas into models, we also gain something. In research we are willing to accept the loss because of the precision and possibility of empirical testing that a formal model allows. Similarly, intermediate modeling can possibly be justified because the modeling provides students who intend to go on in economics with a needed introduction into how economists go about economic analysis.[1]

It is at the principles level that the costs of the multiple translation far exceed the benefits. Ninety-nine percent of principles students are not going on to become economists. We require stories to follow from formal models. In making the formal models accessible to a broad range of students we have so simplified the models that they are vague shadows of the research models economists use to consider the questions. Allowable introductory models can involve nothing beyond tenth-grade algebra, geometry, and logic. This causes three problems.

First, to mathematically sophisticated students, the introductory models look naive and simplistic; these students are discouraged from going into economics because it is too simple. Second, by tying the models to stories we limit the stories we tell. Dynamics, stochastic processes, path dependencies, nonlinear processes—areas where the excitement in economics research is—are all ruled out, or tend to be ignored or downplayed. Third, we generally do not succeed in teaching students the value of formal modeling, or even in teaching them remedial algebra and geometry. The problems are too deep-seated; the mathematical deficiencies built in through years of schooling are not going to be corrected in one course where the primary goal is to teach about the economy. The reality is that these students end up spending most of their time struggling with the math of the models rather than with ideas of the story.

To say that we shouldn't teach introductory students elementary formal models is far too radical a suggestion to have any hope of being considered. Thus, in this chapter, I am proposing a less radical solution—that we separate the two: If we want to teach models, I propose we do so as a type of calisthenics of the mind.[2] I propose that we do not tie our central story line to that formal model, the way we currently do.

Separating the teaching of models from the teaching of the ideas frees us to teach the story of economics within an historical, case study, structure. This alternative structure will let us better relate to students the exciting conundrums with which the top researchers are struggling. It allows us to demonstrate the challenges economists have faced as they have struggled with the problems, and to present the many ideas they have developed to deal with those challenges. Separating the stories we tell from the models we teach will be enormously enabling. It allows us to tell about informal ideas, that cannot be modeled formally, but that excite the imagination.

I will demonstrate the argument in terms of our introductory presentation of growth.

THE CURRENT INTRO GROWTH STORY

Currently we tell the growth story centered around the Solow growth model. In introductory macro we don't teach the Solow growth model explicitly; that would be much too hard for principles students, and, to be honest, is pushing the limits of most intermediate students. But the Solow growth model determines the structure of the way we present growth in introductory courses. It focuses the presentation on the production function, and focuses on the role of savings and investment and diminishing marginal returns. Technological change enters into the story as a supporting idea, which can temporarily overcome the unrelenting pressure of diminishing marginal returns.

If one were interested in telling an exciting story, and, in my view, a more insightful story of growth, the order would be reversed. The dynamic aspects of growth involve technology, and thus technology is the natural center of the introductory story. Similarly, increasing returns, and the many other elements of the economy that can lower costs over time—path dependencies, dynamic feedbacks, and network externalities—replace diminishing marginal returns as the central guiding elements of the story. Investment and saving become supporting ideas. The story line focuses on the tendency of a market economy toward explosive growth, which somehow is held in check by political, physical, and social constraints. We don't tell that story to introductory students because the formal models that incorporate such stories are too complicated.

AN HISTORICAL INTRODUCTION TO GROWTH

I propose that we replace the current model-centered story with a historical-centered story that introduces students to growth through a consideration of the broad historical developments and facts about growth. A natural introduction to the historical approach to growth is the work of Douglass North (North and Thomas, 1973) or Rosenberg and Birdzell (1986). That work shows how growth rates are correlated with the development of markets, and that those growth rates have accelerated over time. Angus Maddison (1999) sums up the historical evidence on growth with a single graph that shows the growth rate from 1000 to the present. In the graph it is clear that: (1) before markets were the main organizing structure of society, growth was minimal; and (2) growth rates have increased over time.

The historical approach centers the growth story around the explanations of these two empirical phenomena. It presents students with the question: Why have markets and growth proceeded together? In answering this question students are directed toward stories involving the division of labor, increasing returns flowing from that division of labor, technological development, and the extent of the market. Markets allow specialization; specialization allows people to focus on what they have a comparative advantage in, and to develop comparative advantages through learning by doing.

THE ROLE OF CASE STUDIES IN THE HISTORICAL APPROACH

Case studies in the historical approach have a different purpose from case studies in a modeling approach. In a modeling approach case studies are examples of principles that students learned in models. In the historical approach case studies are the raw materials from which students derive the principles. In the historical approach one builds up from examples to principles, rather than builds down to cases from principles developed in models. Possible cases include the development of the Swiss watch industry, the industrial revolution in Britain, and recent developments in computer technology in Silicon Valley. One can extrapolate from these cases to central issues in growth such as network externalities, technological change, and decreasing costs. One can show examples of where one technology overtakes another, and emphasize the point that growth often involves new goods replacing old goods, not producing more of the same good. All these issues are hard to fit into the current production function framework.

Building up (with guidance) from case studies is an exciting way to teach that allows students to develop their own principles and insights. Because they have developed the principles themselves, those principles will fit into their mindset, which is the world they are currently experiencing, better than principles developed from abstract models that have no meaning to them.

One does not have to generalize from this case study to a theory; in fact,

Nathan Rosenberg (1994), whose work serves as a model of the historical approach to growth, argues specifically against doing so, since each case is particular. But a case study can be suggestive of certain principles. At our current level of understanding of the growth process, anything other than suggestive propositions would be too much.

SOME DIFFERENCES IN EMPHASES

The historical approach leads to some different emphases than does the current model-based approach. One difference in emphasis is that saving and investment play supporting roles, not the central role given to them by the Solow growth model. In the historical approach, the growth process is a cumulative process; growth creates wealth, which creates the saving, and investment, which fuels the growth. An economy can end up in either a vicious circle or a virtuous circle. There is no foregone conclusion that growth will return to any predetermined growth rate.

A second difference in emphasis is that the discussion of the roles of increasing and decreasing returns is reversed—the main thrust of the historical story is increasing returns and the self-propelling nature of growth. Diminishing returns is de-emphasized. Increasing returns and other factors that lead to lower costs through time dominate the discussion because historically they have done so. In the Solow growth model approach we have to develop the concept of diminishing returns, and then explain why, empirically, diminishing returns have not led to decreased growth rates. We force students to learn technical ideas and then modify them. As they do, they get lost in the models. In the historical approach, we can get right to the elements that have won out in the past.

A third difference concerns efficiency. The historical approach to growth gives far less emphasis to the static concept of efficiency and focuses instead on dynamic efficiency—the role of markets in bringing about innovation and technological change.

A fourth change in emphasis concerns the long-run/short-run division. The model-driven approach emphasizes the separation of the long run and short run. In high-level research, we know that separation is problematic; the two must be tied together, and many of the interesting developments in macro involve the assumption that expectations of what happens in the long run will influence what happens in the short run. In the historical approach an increase in demand could stimulate the economy, and induce innovation that could lead to a continual change in the growth rate. In the Solow growth model, that could not occur.

HISTORICAL PRECEDENT FOR THE HISTORICAL APPROACH

The historical approach to growth is not new. It was the connection between markets and growth that led Adam Smith to write his *Wealth of Nations*. Adam Smith emphasized the division of labor and the general advantages of markets. Markets, by allowing trade, create an environment of growth. In Smith's story the division of labor is mixed with increasing returns to scale, capital accumulation, and learning by doing into a story in which markets lead individuals to create the wealth of nations. Smith's story is one in which the extent of the market, increasing returns, and dynamic feedbacks play central roles.

A SIMULATION APPROACH TO GROWTH

History and case studies get us only so far. I fully agree that to show complex relationships we need to get into formal models. While I do not believe that we can tie the growth story line onto formal models that the introductory students develop from scratch, I do think that we can usefully tie growth stories to pre-digested models, which is essentially what computer simulations are. While simulation involves a lot of math, the math is hidden; all intro students need do is use the computer, which is a skill that students are more likely to have than the math skill necessary to understand a standard model. Roughgarden's (1996) text on ecology provides an example of how the growth story could be presented with simulation models.[3] Simulations allow one to demonstrate open rather than closed models, which lets one talk about certain periods of explosive growth.

One simulation that I use in teaching introductory growth is the Game of Life which, starting from some simple rules, shows a dynamic process can multiply and develop. It provides a foundation for stories with increasing returns and complicated dynamic processes.

The story that these computer simulations, and, in research, agent-based models, emphasize is a different story than the Solow growth model emphasizes. In that Solow model, the economy always returns to the underlying growth rate, as if that rate were somehow a God-given constant. In these computer models fundamental indeterminacy is emphasized. The implied story line is that markets lead to growth because markets allow individuals the possibility to experiment. Experimentation and freedom to try out new things are the driving force of growth. We don't know what causes growth, but what we do know is the institutional environment that is conducive to growth.

CONCLUSION

There are many ways to teach a subject, and it is natural for economists to structure their teaching around formal models. But at the introductory level, that approach makes economics boring to students because they don't know the language of models. By presenting economic ideas in a language with which they are more comfortable, we make introductory economics more exciting for them, and more satisfying for us to teach.

NOTES

1. I qualify this because in liberal arts programs without business schools, most majors are not planning to go into economics; they are planning to go into business.
2. In justifying such "calisthenics models" to students I compare their minds to my body, which is not a hardbody, and suggest that just as physical calisthenics would be useful for my body, mental calisthenics would be useful for their minds.
3. Roughgarden's presentation is at a higher level than I am suggesting here, but it has some excellent, creative approaches of tying simulations with learning about growth.

6. Teaching Keynes in the 21st Century

There has been a lot of discussion lately on what do with Keynesian economics in the principles course. Some new principles books are treating Keynesian economics as an historical artifact, no longer relevant to current economic events.[1] Others, such as McConnell and Brue (1999), continue to make Keynesian economics the core of students' understanding of macro. I come out firmly on the side of saving Keynesian economics, or at least something similar to what we now call Keynesian economics. I'll explain below what I mean by that. For now, let me present the arguments that have been put forward for dumping Keynesian economics. Four reasons are generally suggested:

1. As a guide to policy, the Keynesian model is wrong; it teaches students that deficits expand the economy and surpluses contract the economy. But in the 1990s deficits were contracting, and the economy was booming. Thus, we should abandon the Keynesian model and replace it with a presentation of the long-run relationship between deficits, interest rates, and growth. We should teach that deficits have little effect on, or contract, the economy, emphasizing the Ricardo equivalence theorem.[2]

2. Empirically, multiplier effects aren't very large, and the consumption function is nowhere near as stable as it once seemed. Hence, as a basis for policy, the Keynesian multiplier model is almost unusable. Indeed Robert Barro (1996) goes so far as to argue that the World War II deficit spending isn't even an example of the multiplier working—even though unemployment was reduced from 14 percent to under 2 percent during that time. Barro argues that the economy didn't expand much more than the increase in government spending, so therefore there was no multiplier effect even then, and by induction, if not then, when?

3. The economy gravitates to a long-run natural rate equilibrium on its own. It is not unstable as suggested by the Keynesian model. Thus, we should teach a model based on a concept of the natural rate of unemployment and its corresponding potential income toward which the economy always gravitates.[3]

4. The economy doesn't have cycles any more; hence cycles and stabilization policy are obsolete. Thus, the Keynesian model, which highlights cyclical fluctuations, is also obsolete and should be replaced with a model

of long-run equilibrium growth. On the intermediate level, that model is the Solow growth model; on the principles level it is a general discussion of steady-state growth with essentially no formal model. [4]

WHAT KEYNESIAN ECONOMICS SHOULD BE SAVED?

Although I am arguing that Keynesian economics should be saved, I want to make it clear that I do not want to save everything that has been swept under the Keynesian mantle. I am quite willing to jettison much of what has gone under the name Keynesianism.

I am even willing to admit that a key reason for the decline of Keynesian economics has been the ambiguity about what is meant by Keynesian economics and that much of this ambiguity is traceable to inconsistencies in Keynes' writing. There have been numerous interpretations of Keynes, all supported by references to the literature. The debates resulting from these various interpretations have consumed a large portion of many brilliant researchers' time. I avoid those debates completely. Quite honestly, I don't care what Keynes said when and I don't care whether what I call Keynesianism is what Keynes really meant, and I don't think students care either. I'm not even sure that Keynes really knew what he meant.

But that said, there was clearly something there in Keynes' writings, and in what goes under the name Keynesianism in the principles textbooks, that I believe is worth preserving and teaching to students. What is that something? To me, it is a vision of macroeconomics that differs from the vision that has become known as the Classical vision. Specifically, *it is a vision that does not assume that the market economy—left to its own devices—will necessarily gravitate toward a preferable equilibrium.* That is, it is the acceptance of the proposition that the economy is complex and that, theoretically, markets may not always lead to the optimal aggregate results. A person who accepts my interpretation of Keynesianism accepts that the market can, at times, gravitate toward an undesirable equilibrium for a period of time long enough to warrant the consideration of government action to modify that equilibrium.

Although I was never taught so in my principles course, a subset of Classical economists fully accepted this vision, at least as being a possibility. It was only later, after I became interested in the development of ideas and read the Classics in this light, that I learned that there was much more to Classical economics than I had been taught. What I was taught was that Classical economics was wrong and that Keynesian economics was the truth. What I was taught was a model that demonstrated that the aggregate economy was unstable—that is, if it deviated from its potential income, there was no natural tendency for it to return to that equilibrium. The macroeconomy needed direct government intervention to stabilize it. Keynesian economics was presented as a scientific truth to be contrasted with the Classical incorrect way of looking at the world. That brand of mechanical Keynesianism ended long ago, and I am pleased that it did.

But, recently, it seems that the pendulum has swung too far the other way. Now it is the subset of the Classical vision that sees the unimpeded market as the solution to all our problems that is being taught as the scientific truth, and it is Keynesian economics that is being relegated to the dustbin of history. It is this tendency of macroeconomics texts to swing from one extreme to another that underlies the joke about the student who comes to visit the professor he had 25 years ago. Looking at the exam the professor is about to give he remarks that it is precisely the same exam that he was given 25 years ago. The professor responds that that is true; in economics, the questions always remain the same; it's the answers that change.

What I am arguing for is teaching macroeconomics without the pendulum—for us to teach that there is a tendency for the market to work fine on its own, and for private institutions to adjust to the problems that develop. We also need to teach that, at times, the macro economy can experience serious coordination problems that may require government action.[5] To do all, that we need to teach both what is currently seen as the Classical model, and simultaneously teach the Keynesian model with the multiplier analysis that shows how reverberations from an initial shock can lead the economy to an undesirable position. Economic theory does not tell us what model is appropriate to what time period. That is a matter of judgment, and in that judgment reasonable economists may differ.

I believe that the large majority of economists would find this middle ground acceptable. But it is hard to stay on this middle ground. One of the reasons is that the two alternative views have not been allowed to coexist on the level of high theory. The debate about which of the two views is correct has filled hundreds of thousands of pages of journal articles, 99.9 percent of which are irrelevant to principles students. Specifically, at the principles level all the debates about what might happen if there were instantaneous price-level flexibility, all the esoteric debates about wealth effects, and all the debates about whether Keynesianism was a theoretical or a practical revolution are beside the point.

Again, Keynes is partially to blame for this state of affairs. To distinguish his view from the Classical economists' view, which also allowed that less than instantaneous wage and price adjustment could cause coordination problems, Keynes made his case assuming a perfectly competitive goods market. His policy arguments would have followed just as well if he had simply stated that institutionally wages and prices do not adjust instantaneously, and that these institutions require a price level that does not fluctuate "too much." If you assume some degree of wage and price-level stability is required by the institutional core of a monetary economy, then that debate about what would happen if there were perfect price–level flexibility becomes irrelevant.

In my view, all principles students need know is that there is such a debate, and that economics theory does not lead to a definitive conclusion about whether the economy gravitates toward a unique equilibrium within a politically acceptable period of time. To convey this to students the principles have only to point out that in the real world wages and prices tend to adjust less than instantaneously and, in such a world, repercussions of effects of one market can influence other markets and lead the economy to undesirable outcomes.

This is not a highly controversial position. Monetarists would agree with it; and many of Keynes' Classical contemporaries—the economists of the 1920s and 1930s—would also agree with it. In fact, about the only people who will disagree with it are a few purely theoretical new Classical and real-business-cycle economists. Consider the following quotation:

> In the first place my attention is fixed by the inquiry, so important to the present interests of society: What is the cause of the general glut of all the markets in the world, to which merchandise is incessantly carried to be sold at a loss? What is the reason that in the interior of every state, notwithstanding a desire of action adapted to all the developments of industry, there exists universally a difficulty of finding lucrative employments? And when the cause of this chronic disease is found, by what means is it to be remedied? On these questions depend the tranquillity and happiness of nations.

Who do you think said it? As Petur Jonsson (1995) pointed out, it was Jean Baptiste Say, the Say of Say's Law (Say, 1821, p. 2). Keynes set up Say as the straw man of Classical economics in order to tear Classical economics down, but the real Say was a subtle writer who fully believed general gluts were possible. Another leading monetary economist of Keynes' time, Denis Robertson, had a sequence model of the economy that arrived at Keynesian-type results, as did Lauchlin Currie here in the United States. What I am saying is that it is a textbook fiction initially perpetrated by Keynes that led us to the polar views of Keynesian economics and Classical economics. Keynes wanted to differentiate his product and he did so by painting Classical economists as one-dimensional and believing in something that many did not believe in.

The reality is that Classical economics had an extremely rich and varied tradition that included much, if not all, of what we currently present as Keynesian economics. In marketing his ideas Keynes took that rich and varied tradition and pigeonholed it into a one-dimensional line of thought that he centered around Say's Law. As I have argued in *The Coming of Keynesianism to America* (1996, p. 15), in doing so he unfairly characterized Classical economics. Had Keynesianism not existed, much of what we teach as Keynesian economics would still be taught, only it wouldn't be called Keynesian. Thus, the reason I oppose dumping Keynesian economics has nothing to do with dumping the Keynesian name. The reason is that the profession's proponents of dumping Keynesian economics try to swing the pendulum back too far toward an implicit assumption that the market solves all our problems, and are leaving out another important pragmatic dimension of Classical thought— the belief that serious problems can develop. For example, in the early 1930s both Frank Knight and A.C. Pigou were supporting government works programs and deficit spending to expand the economy. Similarly Keynes supported public works programs before he wrote the *General Theory*. Even the Austrian economist, W.H. Hutt, one of the strongest anti-Keynesians, writes, "But once the persistent ignoring of 'classical' precepts had precipitated chaos, and insurmountable political problems obviously block the way to non-inflationary recovery, only a pedant would oppose inflation" (1979, p. 45).

Most Classical economists didn't believe that *theoretically* the market was the solution to our problems—that view only developed in the analytic revolution when economists became enamored of math. Most Classical economists believed that, *practically*, the market was the best way to solve our problems. Generally, I believe that Classical view is right, as did Keynes. But it is not always the case, and students need to be taught that. They need to be taught that the argument for leaving things to the market is an historical argument, not a theoretical argument. It is based on the importance of government failure, not the absence of market failure.

With that background discussion, let me now return to the four reasons for dumping the Keynesian model discussed at the beginning of the chapter.

1.	The first reason was that as a guide to policy, the Keynesian model is wrong. But that view is based on seeing the Keynesian model we present to principles students as a mechanistic, rather than an interpretative, model. The interpretative Keynesian model does not say that deficit spending will always expand the economy. In fact nowhere in the *General Theory* will you find an argument that deficit spending is needed to keep the economy going.

	As I point out in "Was Keynes a Keynesian or a Lernerian?" (1984), Keynes was strongly against deficits. Keynesian economics simply states that deficits may be helpful at times. And that, I think, is true. At times they may be. I am not the only one who believes that. In policymakers' minds, demand-management policy, taken broadly, and not as a tool of fine tuning, is alive and well in policy discussions. We are doing our students a disservice if we do not teach them the multiplier model upon which that view is based. If we are teaching what policymakers talk about, which is what I think we should teach, policymakers think that multiplier effects are important. Consider Japan's macro policy discussion in the late 1990s of tax cuts and spending programs. Clearly, policymakers still discuss macroeconomics in Keynesian terms.

What was happening in the 1990s to our economy was not a contradiction of the Keynesian model, but, rather, an example of it. For one thing, the price level remained constant even as the economy expanded beyond what economists believed possible. Think back: The reason the Keynesian model was dumped was that the assumption it made about fixed prices over a range of output did not seem to hold. But if you look at the economy today, it fits the assumption of the Keynesian model. And now that it fits, we're dumping it.

Even the expected surplus is consistent with the interpretative Keynesian model. Keynes emphasized the uncertainty in the economy and fully believed that expansions in consumer and investment spending could fuel a substantial boom. And that is what happened in the late 1990s. The expenditure function has shifted up quite independently, causing tax revenue to increase and thereby causing a budget surplus.

2. The second argument is that empirically, multiplier effects aren't very large. The evidence here is ambiguous, especially if monetary and fiscal policy are thought of within a forward-looking expectational model. In such a model the mere expectation of the policy can affect decisions and affect the economy, making it almost impossible to measure empirically what the actual effect of the policy is.

What should be deleted from the model is any underlying certainty about the size of multipliers. That's why I favor teaching the interpretative, not the mechanistic, Keynesian model. The interpretative Keynesian model uses the multiplier model simply to suggest direction of policy effects, not to be interpreted literally. It is an exercise of the mind, not a model of the economy.[6]

If we don't teach the interpretative multiplier model, students are left with the story that the economy adjusts to shocks and never can experience unwanted booms or busts. That, in my view, is not correct, nor is it what policymakers believe.

All real-world econometric macro models have multiplier effects in them. For example, the DRI model is centered around demand equations and cost-plus markups and has an implicit multiplier of about 2. Why? Because that is the model that empirically best fits our economy.

Finally, let me turn to Barro's argument about the size of the multiplier in World War II. It is true that there were no significant multiplier effects beyond the initial spending of government. But the reason why is clear. The government imposed rationing, and a whole set of programs, such as price controls, to stop the secondary effects, because it wanted to focus all the production towards the war effort.

3.   The third reason—the gravitation toward the natural rate argument— also has a problem. We economists simply don't know what the natural rate is, if there is one. Consider our record. How many economists in the early 1990s predicted that in the late 1990s US inflation would be less than 2 percent and unemployment less than 4.5 percent? Few. Let me present some economists' views, emphasizing that these were generally held beliefs of economists, and the economists chosen are only examples. The first example is Robert Gordon who in 1994 advised the Federal Reserve Board that the natural rate was probably 6 percent and possibly as high as 6.5 percent. In 1995 he adjusted that to 5.5 percent, and when it went lower, lowered his estimate to 5 percent. Another example is Edmund Phelps, who in 1994 was saying that the natural rate was 6.5 percent; he lowered his estimate to 6 percent in 1995 and thereafter made no estimates for the record that I know of.[7] The final example I will give comes from a series of statements by Stuart Weiner, vice president of the Kansas City Fed. In 1993 he wrote:

> . . . estimates suggest that the natural rate of unemployment is currently near 6.25 percent and could move even higher depending upon the extent and persistence of structural disruptions. . . . Thus, the near-term inflation risk may be higher than generally perceived. (p. 53)

Fact: Unemployment rate in 1993 was 6.5 percent at the time the article was written. Core inflation rate was about 3.2 percent in 1993 and fell to 2.7 percent in 1994.

In 1994 he said:

> . . . the natural rate is currently 6.25 percent. With the actual unemployment rate averaging 6.2 percent in the second quarter, this means that labor markets currently are operating at full capacity. (p. 6)

Fact: Unemployment rate in 1994 was 6.1 percent at the time the article was written. Core inflation rate was about 2.7 percent in 1994 and 3.0 percent in 1995.

Not to be undone, in 1995 he said that the natural rate was 6.25 percent and continued:

> . . . I do not find the skeptics' arguments compelling. If I had to choose just one variable to help me forecast inflation turning points, it would be the

unemployment gap. And that gap is signaling that concerns about future inflationary pressures are well founded. (p. 24)

Fact: Unemployment rate in 1995 was 5.6 percent at the time the article was written. Core inflation rate was about 3.0 percent in 1995 and fell to 2.8 percent in 1996.

No further articles by Weiner on the natural rate appear in the *Federal Reserve Bank of Kansas City Economic Review*. In 1999, unemployment, when this chapter was written, was below 4.5 percent and inflationary pressures continued to subside. I want to reemphasize that Weiner is not alone; he was expressing the view, based on the best empirical evidence available to them, of the large majority of economists in the 1990s. Not surprisingly, most economists are now far more circumspect when talking about the natural rate. My question is: Do we really want to make a fixed natural rate the centerpiece of our presentation of macro?

4.   Lastly let me turn to the fourth reason: The economy does not have cycles any more; we are on an upward growth path that will continue into the indefinite future. In response I simply cite the Asian crisis of the late 1990s. Was that an experience of economies on their natural rate growth path? No, it was a crisis of confidence that affected the economies and brought about recession in those countries.

I, for one, would not want to go on record as saying that the US economy is recession-proof. The reality is that there is a lot we don't know about the macro economy—generally it is relatively stable, but because it is based on financial stability, and that is based on trust and expectations, the stability can erode quickly.

CONCLUSION

There's a lot we don't know about the macro economy. We should not be embarrassed by that. The macro economy is complicated—very complicated— and it is not surprising that we have a poor record of predicting. But given that we don't know a lot, shouldn't we be honest with our students, and not present macroeconomics as understanding more than it does?

What concerns me about the direction of principles of economics textbooks in the United States is that in the attempt to simplify, they are presenting economic knowledge as more certain than it is. In doing that they are giving up teaching the economic method, and, instead, concentrating on teaching what the policy answers are. The truth is we don't know for sure what the policy answers are. US economists did not predict the growth the US economy is currently experienced in the late 1990s, and we have been particularly unsuccessful in predicting which areas would grow.

In thinking about what to teach there is another legacy that I think we can usefully gain from Keynes. Specifically, Keynes was well known for his changing views. Hence the famous joke—if you have four economists you will have four different positions, unless of course one of them is Mr. Keynes; then you will have seven different positions.[8] This was true because Keynes was a pragmatist about policy, who drew his policy views from several different models. He was a student of Marshall, and he said, "The theory of economics is a method rather than a doctrine, an apparatus of the mind, a technique of thinking which helps its possessor to draw correct conclusions" (Keynes, 1921, p. v).

This quotation is the epitome of the Marshallian method. It tells us to use economics as an engine of analysis, not as a set of principles. If we keep that Marshallian method in mind, we will be giving our students a good foundation in understanding macroeconomics and we will be treating Keynes the way he should be treated—as an economist who carried on an important tradition in Classical economics.

NOTES

1. This tendency is most pronounced in Mankiw (1998).
2. Robert Barro (1996) argues this position most strongly, but it can be found in many intermediate texts such as Hall and Taylor (1997).
3. This view can be found in almost all intermediate and introductory textbooks. See either Mankiw (1998) or Hall and Taylor (1997) as examples.
4. Mankiw (1998) starts his introductory book with a presentation of long-run growth; in intermediate macro books Hall and Taylor (1997) and Dornbush, Fisher and Startz (1999), both have changed their presentation to emphasize the Solow growth model.
5. The term "coordination problems" comes from game theory and is based on the possibility of multiple equilibria. The economy will arrive at an equilibrium but it may not be the most desirable equilibrium. In macro what is meant is that expectational conundrums can develop that lead the economy to an equilibrium at other than the desirable output. See Colander (1996), for a further discussion.
6. For a further discussion of what is meant by "interpretative model", see Colander (1998).
7. For a discussion of these, and other economists', predictions of the natural rate see Amanda Bennett (1996).
8. As usual, Keynes had a retort. When challenged for his inconsistency he replied that when he was presented with new evidence he changed his mind. Then he asked in turn what he did when he was faced with new evidence.

PART IV

Doing Art in the Current Institutional Setting

7. Confessions of an Economic Gadfly[*]

How do I work? Hard and long. Why do I do it? I don't know, but then there are many things I do for reasons unknown. Actually, I am not totally the directionless, clueless, person the above answer suggests. I have a number of conjectures about why I work hard and long. One is that I'm an inquisitive person who, like my eight-year-old, keeps asking "Why?" until I come up with *an answer that satisfies me*. Combine that inquisitiveness with a dogged persistence that abhors fudges in answers unless they are called what they are—fudges—and you have the makings of a gadfly like myself.

THE YEAH CRITERION

In explaining what I mean by "an answer that satisfies me" I could discuss the nature of satisfaction, the Duhem Quine Thesis, proofs, refutations, and lines of demarcation in this chapter, but that would be misleading since what I mean by "satisfy" is guttural, not intellectual. A satisfactory explanation for me involves an inner sense—an intuition—which tells me "Yeah, that's right; that's the way it works." I will call it the "Yeah criterion." For an intuitive economist the "Yeah criterion" is central.[1]

In no way am I saying that the Yeah criterion is a criterion of truth. I recognize that what makes sense to me is structured by my training, my biases, and my vision of the world. As I learn more, my common sense changes and what is a satisfying explanation changes—sometimes the unsatisfying becomes satisfying, and sometimes the unsatisfying becomes more unsatisfying. For that reason the Yeah criterion is not a stand-alone criterion; for it to work requires an understanding of the literature and the thinking of both past and present experts. As I read the literature I often discover that some problems that have bothered me have bothered researchers before me. This is why the history of thought and literature studies have been so central to my study of economics. In earlier writers I can often find pointed discussions of the problems I am having with the intuition, and explanations of why they did what they did.

INTUITION, EGO, AND THE YEAH CRITERION

For the Yeah criterion to work, one needs an enormous ego, and an ability not to be influenced by the crowd. Most non-egotistical people will reason, often implicitly, that if an explanation is good enough for the enormously bright individuals who have considered an issue previously, it is good enough for them. In considering issues, I try to keep such reasonable considerations from my mind, and avoid letting other people's acceptance of an argument—either positively or negatively—influence my consideration of that issue.

For example, the standard cost curve analysis in the textbooks does not meet the Yeah criterion for me, and I have been working off and on for the past 20 years to understand why it doesn't in a way that I can explain to others. My intuition tells me that Jacob Viner's famous mistake—telling the draftsman to do the impossible—was not a mistake, but was instead a misunderstanding by Viner about the existence of discontinuities as one moved from the long to the short period.[2] Viner wanted a smooth transition between the two, while his intuition was dealing with discrete jumps. If I am correct, Viner's recantation was misplaced, and a reconsideration of the structural aspects of the basic model of the firm will make his goof no goof at all. That reconsideration will give us a better understanding of numerous microeconomic issues.

The standard AS/AD analysis is another analysis that did not meet my Yeah criterion and my continued attacking of the standard AS/AD analysis (most recently, Colander, 1995) has led many economists to consider me non-mainstream. But, if accepted (a big if), my reinterpretation of AS/AD analysis will play a role in changing the profession's thinking about what the central aspects of the Keynesian revolution are.

I have no great sense that acceptance of my ideas is imminent; changing established beliefs, especially when they are deeply built in and little thought about, is not easy; it requires a strong reliance on, and belief in, one's understanding. I expect most gadflies rely heavily on their egos and their Yeah criteria.

THE MIT AND CHICAGO APPROACHES TO ECONOMICS

I think the majority of people in the world approach understanding using something similar to my "Yeah" approach. Most contemporary economists, at least in their stated methodology, don't, which is why I am considered a gadfly. Actually, I should clarify the above statement since the intuitive approach is often associated with the Chicago approach to economics, and, while that Chicago approach is in decline, it is still around, especially at the introductory level of economics. In fact, I suspect that many people are attracted to economics because of its ability to give one "Yeah" highs. (This is especially true of those who learn "Chicago economics" early on, as I did.)

I quite agree that Chicago economics is wonderful at producing superficial Yeah highs. In fact, if you really get into the Chicago model, you have the Yeah sense for everything you look at. A well-trained Chicago economist can explain everything with a simple economic model.

But like many highs, for most people the highs from the simple economic model wear off, and doubts start emerging. The problem is the Chicago model explains too much. There are other factors that are determining what happens, which should fit into the explanation, but don't. When this realization hit me, as it did in my junior year in college, I was ruined as a Chicago economist. I had lost the faith.

I believe something similar happened to the economics profession over the last seventy-five years. The non-mathematical intuitive approach lost favor as it became associated with laissez-faire policy recommendations that were claimed to arise from economic theory. The claim that laissez-faire policy conclusions followed from economic theory did not fit an informed person's Yeah criterion. But since many intuitive economists said they did, economic researchers went about showing formally that the intuitive economists were claiming far too much for their intuition and for laissez faire.[3]

As this formal work showed the major failings of earlier economists' intuition, formal work acquired a higher and higher stature. Intuitive understanding based on informal models was looked down upon. For lack of a better term I call this formal approach "the MIT approach." It understands the economy through simple, but formal, models. In the 1990s this MIT approach replaced the Chicago intuitive approach except in a few market niches. (With the death of George Stigler, and with Milton Friedman having moved to the Hoover Institute, the MIT approach has even largely replaced the Chicago approach at Chicago.)

Thus, in the 1990s the MIT approach was the mainstream economic approach, and any intuitive approach to understanding economic issues that carries over from the early economic courses (one of the niches where the Chicago approach still is strong) is frowned upon and discouraged. Most economists have it brainwashed out of their minds. Those few who do not succumb to the brainwashing, and who continue to approach economics using the Yeah criterion, are selected out of the profession by the institutions that determine who advances and who doesn't. The Yeah criterion doesn't cut it with most journal editors or tenure committees.

The MIT approach is, in my view, sterile and highly limiting for most economists. By eliminating, or at least significantly surpressing, the Yeah criterion, it eliminates the passion in doing economics and instead directs economists' goals toward financial gain and institutional success. Economics becomes a job, not a vocation.

The above discussion will get me in hot water with both Chicago and MIT economists. Chicago economists will argue that their approach has no ideological slant, and MIT economists will argue that the MIT training does not diminish intuition—it simply tries to raise the level of intuition to a higher level. I won't dispute either side here, other than to say that an approach must be judged not by what its best practitioners say it is, but by its fruits—what does the standard person trained in that tradition come away with. Judged by their consequences, I have no trouble with either of the above judgments, nor do I think a neutral observer will have a problem with them. In fact, Robert Solow has said as much—that the problem with economists today is that they don't use their intuition enough (Solow, 1994). I agree. What Solow will object to is my argument that it is the MIT training that has eliminated that intuitive approach.

Let me give an example of what the MIT approach does. A while back I went to dinner with some economics professors. At dinner I was describing the reasoning behind the market anti-inflation plan that Abba Lerner and I had been working on. An MIT-trained economist asked me if I had a formal model of it, and when I said "No," he said that he couldn't discuss it. For him, the Yeah criterion was irrelevant; understanding had to go through a prism of a formal model. In the MIT approach the standard student comes away with a belief that if an issue doesn't have a formal model, it cannot be discussed or thought about.

When I have pushed MIT economists on the role of intuition, they agree with me that economists should be able to deal with issues on an informal intuitive level, and those who cannot are bad economists. They point to economists such as Paul Krugman and George Akerlof who combine both an informal intuitive approach and the MIT approach. I agree, Paul and George are superb economists. They can rise above the models, because they have superb intuitions, and a different vision from many other economic researchers. But they both play the game by MIT rules. What's modelable guides their research and their intuition. They have made important contributions, but imagine what they could do if their intuitions were freed from the formal modeling shackles.

I think that contrasting my approach to studying economic problems with that given by Paul Krugman in his essay "How I Work" (Szenberg, 1998, pp. 143–52), is a useful way of seeing the difference between my approach and what I would call the best of the MIT approach. I'm the extreme opposite of Paul. Modelability, for me, is a technical issue to be dealt with only after one has chosen what to study by the Yeah criterion. It's a way of demonstrating, checking, and refining what one already "knows." I deal with ideas on an intuitive level, not on a formal model level. Formal modeling, for me, is useful to answer fine points, not to create and understand theory.

Paul follows the MIT approach; he understands things such as the importance of non-linearities and increasing returns, and then puts them to the model criteria. If the work doesn't make the model criteria, it doesn't meet his understanding criteria. That's why many intuitive economists don't see Paul's work as innovative, and they see him as claiming far more originality for his work than it deserves. In the MIT approach, he is correct; in the intuitive approach his critics are correct. I follow the intuitive approach and put existing models to the intuitive understanding criteria. If a model doesn't make intuitive sense it must be wrong, and I focus my work on explaining why.

Simple formal models that MIT economists find so enlightening often grate on my intuition. True, they may be an improvement on an existing simple formal model, but often they merely add one new twist formally—a twist that informal, intuitive, economists have long understood. Moreover, often the intuitive economist will have recognized that the relevance of this particular twist can only be understood by adding seven or eight additional twists concurrently. The MIT approach doesn't see an issue in an alternative way unless it is in a formal model, whereas I see any simple formal model as far too limiting to the twists I intuitively believe are necessary.

In short, I do not believe that most of the economic events I am analyzing can be explained by a simple formal model without the addition of enormous institutional detail that simple formal models cannot accommodate. Krugman argues the MIT line that we should "simplify, simplify." I follow Einstein— "Models should be as simple as possible, *but not more so*." My vision of the economy is one of complexity, and any explanation that fits my Yeah criterion must incorporate that complexity, or at least tell me why the complexity isn't going to affect the analysis. When I try to conceive of a general mathematical statement of the economic problem, I come up with an extraordinarily complicated set of interrelated dynamic equations that lead to chaotic, super-nonlinear dynamic models.

The MIT vision sees it as possible to reduce that chaos—without formally modeling the institutions—to simple formal models with linear dynamics, and deterministic results. They have to do so to arrive at a tractable model. Tractability runs roughshod over intuition, and creates a set of models that, for me, do not meet the Yeah criterion. The only way I can see an economy such as ours as working is with institutions limiting changes and creating some stability out of chaos. Somehow in the process of educating children enormous limitations on individuals' choices are placed on them by institutions and social pressures. Society shapes us, child and adult, to fit into a workable marketplace. Whenever I see analyses—such as the standard analyses of production or of distribution—that don't include that shaping process and the institutions that play such an important role in shaping us, I cringe. I cringe a lot when reading economics.

THE POSSIBILITY OF TRADE BETWEEN HIGH-LEVEL THEORISTS AND INTUITIVE ECONOMISTS

The problem with simple formal models is that formal models constrain one's intuition. They embody within them implicit assumptions that one doesn't even know exist. The mathematics one uses in those models is a language and languages are limiting. There are two ways to confront this problem. One way is to delve deeper and deeper into the math—dealing with the complex issues in a highly abstract way so that the few implicit assumptions that remain are clear. Some of the complex game-theoretic work fits this approach, as does some of the recent work on chaos and nonlinear dynamics. At those levels one can integrate one's intuition with formal modeling and the results can be impressive. The models that such economists develop are far from the simple policy-oriented MIT models that Krugman exalts; these are models that have no policy implications because either they generally have no analytic solution —at least not yet—or they are so abstract that they have no obvious relation to reality.

Relating such abstract, formal models with real-world observations is extraordinarily difficult, and for most people, impossible. Thus, while I try to follow the work of modern researchers such as William Brock, and look to it for inspiration, I make no pretense of dealing at that level myself. I go to the other extreme and deal informally with loose ideas that better fit observed reality, and which oftentimes hide logical relationships. Such specialization opens up the possibility of trade, and ideally economics would have two types of economic researchers making trades—formal theorists dealing with highly complex and abstract analysis almost devoid of institutions, and intuitive institutionally-based theorists dealing with real-world institutions and informal abstract analysis. The MIT approach of simple formal models would make sense if there were not increasing returns to scale in research, but it seems obvious that there are increasing returns, so not to take advantage of them and not to encourage specialization is, in my view, a highly inefficient approach to understanding. If you are going to be formally abstract, then go all the way and don't let the real-world issues contaminate the purity of your analysis. If you are going to be concerned with the real world, don't formalize more than the least precise real-world element. To do so is to violate the law of significant digits.

To make sure that I am being clear, and to get me in as much trouble as possible, let me state my position more bluntly. I would say that the MIT economics approach has played an important role in bringing economics to its current sterility. I say this regretfully because I also believe that MIT economics has played a significantly positive role and that it was necessary to get the blatant ideological aspects of earlier intuitive economics out of the models.

MY ROAD TO BECOMING A GADFLY

Having arrived at the view of simple formal models described above, I found myself in a difficult position in my graduate work in economics. I did fine in the mathematics they taught us, but I was not an ultra-mathematician, and did not want to be one. I had been attracted to economics by the intuitive understanding it gave me of events, and its ability to supply me with Yeah highs. But I had rejected the Chicago Creed that the market was inherently good and beyond question.

Faced with my disillusionment with both the Chicago approach and the MIT approach I was in a bind—a bind that I resolved initially by not considering it. Instead, I focused on more immediate concerns, such as getting my dissertation done and getting a job. That meant following the MIT approach, which, interpreted down to a third year graduate student level, meant that the best, quickest, way to a dissertation was to take a simple, formal model and permute it.

Optimal taxation was hot at the time, and Ned Phelps and Bill Vickrey, two of the most interesting professors of economics then at Columbia, were interested in it. So it seemed like a good idea to write a dissertation on optimal taxation, especially since they would allow me to write three essays which I could easily translate into articles. The math in my essays would look impressive and the topic was hot. It was the perfect combination for a thesis. It wasn't a very good thesis, but I soon had two essays done, and was working on the third. That was in 1974; I was on my way to becoming a mainstream economist.

The decision to become a gadfly was made, as are most decisions, in a sequentially rational way. I took the first step along the path later in 1974, when one of those defining events of one's life happened. Although I had suppressed my intuitive approach to economics, I had not totally annihilated it, and one day I was sitting around thinking about inflation, trying to understand why we were having so much inflation and what could be done about it, when I conceived of an economy in which there were property rights in prices.[4] In such an economy individuals wanting to change their own nominal price would pay someone else to change their nominal price in the opposite direction. Only relative price changes would be allowed in such an economy; inflation would be impossible. It was an intriguing idea to me since it allowed the society to control the price level, but it left all relative prices free to fluctuate.

The idea led to numerous questions such as: What price would these rights to change price sell for? and: How would that price vary with change in aggregate demand? I played around with the idea in my mind for a while, and one afternoon sat down and wrote it up in a piece I called "The Free Market Solution to Inflation." I sent copies around to a few people, including Bill Vickrey. I soon got a letter back from Bill (with a copy to my chair) telling me the idea was brilliant. Now it isn't often that one gets such a letter from one's advisor who himself is an innovative economist, and it led me to make a fateful decision: to dump my thesis on optimal taxation (which was almost finished) and to expand this short paper on the free market solution into a thesis.

Actually, the decision wasn't quite so gutsy as it sounds; I explained the situation to Vickrey and asked him if he thought I could finish a thesis on the topic in a year, the time I needed to have it done if I was to stay at Vassar where I was then teaching. He said I could. I then went to Phelps and told him that Vickrey believed I could expand the paper into a thesis in a year, and asked if he felt it was a reasonable plan. He also said yes. So essentially, I had gotten tentative approval from both my advisors before I began.

And a good thing, too, because a year later, when I handed in my thesis, it was done, but it was not very good. The title was "Microeconomic Stabilization Policy for an Economy with Simultaneous Inflation and Unemployment." It was provocative and imaginative; it was also vague, incoherent in parts, and incomplete in others. Still, they let me through, perhaps because they had made almost no criticisms when I handed in successive drafts. Whether this was because they hadn't had the time to read the drafts carefully, or because they didn't know how to comment on such a vague and incoherent thesis, I don't know.

The only real hurdle I faced was my oral defense, and luckily for me, one of the outside examiners was a well-known philosopher who cared little about formal economic models. At the beginning of the defense he suggested that the rules be changed—that the thesis looked like something Vickrey had worked out and that we should have Vickrey, not me, defend it. This provoked laughter and pleasant discussion, leaving little room for piercing questions.

I suspect that thesis decision set me on my gadfly path, because while the thesis wasn't much, it contained the seeds of the ideas for most of my later work. Many of those seeds are still germinating, which gives you an idea of how incomplete the thesis was.

The chance to plant the seeds of new ways of looking at problems is something that few modern economists have, and I am eternally grateful to Bill Vickrey and the almost-directionless Columbia Ph.D. program for allowing me that chance.

Of course, seeds of ideas aren't going to get one a job, so I still had the job problem to deal with. I should have been scared to death, but in my immaturity, and with my almost total lack of knowledge about the system, I wasn't. After all, Vickrey had told me my paper was brilliant, and when I asked if he thought I could get it published in a top journal, he had responded, "Yes—no problem." I started to get worried when I got my first rejection (from the AER); it wasn't even polite. It said, essentially, that the paper was garbage, poorly written, incomprehensible, and wrong. After a couple more rejections, I began to suspect that I was in trouble, and that maybe that fateful step into following, and trying to develop, my intuition was a step into a deep abyss.

I began to consider other options. I was selected as a Brookings Policy Fellow and went on leave from Vassar to work at the Government Accounting Office on cost analysis, one of the many areas my thesis had touched on. I did a study there that argued essentially that, technically, it was impossible to distinguish a fee from a tax, and that when handing out limited entitlements, one had to base the fees on scarcity costs, not on costs as they were currently being interpreted in the law.

I further argued that when scarce entitlements were involved, costs could only be defined in relation to demand—since the value of the scarce resource was determined by demand. Demand elasticities had to be taken into account in allocating joint costs. While my arguments made good economic sense, they were not what most politicians wanted to hear, and I quickly discovered that I did not have the temperament to play the political economy game in government. So much for that option.

I suspect that many gadflies arrive at a similar stage in their careers, and leave the profession. I certainly considered leaving it, and at that point I seriously considered going to work for a management consultant firm. The pay was much better, and the likelihood of success much higher. I might well have done that too, had it not been for Sidney Weintraub and Abba Lerner.

WITH A LOT OF HELP FROM FRIENDS

While a Brookings Policy Fellow I intermittently continued my work on my free market solution to inflation, but it wasn't going anywhere fast. I gathered another couple of nasty rejections, which told me what I now knew very well— that the paper didn't have the right form—that it talked about an idea without a formal model! I now knew that such an idea was not allowed in any mainstream journal. It was then that I began considering non-mainstream outlets.

One place I looked was to the Post-Keynesians. Sidney Weintraub, together with Henry Wallich, had a TIP (tax-based incomes policy) proposal that was something like my free market solution to inflation. The difference was that theirs was a tax-based policy, and mine was a market-based policy. Theirs was designed as a policy that would work; mine was designed as a theoretical policy with no concern about how it would work out in practice. Sidney was also editor of the *Journal of Post Keynesian Economics,* and as a last resort I sent my paper there. He did not reject it outright, but he did reject it as too abstract, and too theoretical. He suggested I write a new paper which empha-sized TIP more, and then touched on my idea of a market plan. I jumped at the chance, and got a paper accepted. My academic life was not a total failure.

I met Sidney later, and liked him personally, but on economics we didn't agree on many issues. There were major differences in our thinking about anti-inflation policy; he was concerned about practical matters and my con-cern was about the way nominal price-setting institutions could be integrated into a general equilibrium system: thus his analysis of TIP was partial equilib-rium; mine was general equilibrium. He also focused on wages and he took it as given that a wage/price markup had been, and would remain, constant. My proposal focused on value added, and I argued that one couldn't take any wage/price markup as constant when imposing a policy affecting wages. De-spite our differences, Sidney was generally supportive. I think it is important to note that gadflies exist in the profession only because of nurturing by econo-mists such as Sidney. I will be forever grateful to him.

The second fortuitous event was a seminar that Brookings held on TIP, which occurred because Art Okun was there and was interested in TIP. Unfor-tunately, I was not asked to prepare anything since Art saw my work as off in left field. He was concerned with politics and getting something implemented. He felt, I suspect rightly since his political instincts were impeccable, that my discussion of a new market in some abstract concept would have killed the practical hopes for the TIP plan. His focus was on policy. I was disappointed.

Nonetheless, that Brookings seminar was another turning point in my career. The reason was that Abba Lerner came, I think almost uninvited, and discussed what he called WIP (Wage Incomes Policy). This proposal was very similar to mine in that it was a proposal to control inflation by creating property rights. A major difference was that his proposal was a modification of the wage-based TIPs and hence it focused on wages, not prices. A second difference was that he was interested primarily in practical issues (to the degree that Abba could be concerned about practical issues), while I was interested in the underlying theory and what it implied for macroeconomic theorizing.

After the seminar, Ned Phelps introduced me to Abba and told him I had a proposal somewhat similar to his. Abba nodded. Actually, I believe, I had sent

Abba a copy of my early proposal, but I doubt he had read it, or if he had, that he had thought much about it. A couple of days later Abba was on the program at the Eastern Economic Association meetings and I decided to attend; we spoke briefly and I outlined the differences between my proposal and his. He was pleasant, but otherwise noncommittal.

The next time I saw Abba was at the AEA meetings in Chicago. TIP was politically hot then, and there was a session with Abba, Sidney, and Henry Wallich, who was on the Fed board. The room, which held 300 or so, was full; I sat there listening, depressed that my work was being ignored. At the end of the session I got recognized by the chair and asked Abba three questions that I felt showed the weaknesses of his analysis and the strengths of mine. One seldom gets answers at such events, and I didn't, but at least I had had my say, and I felt better for it.

I was presenting a paper on the general topic at the last session of the meetings. There were two people in the audience—friends of the presenters. But then, right after the beginning of the session, in walked Abba. He sat down and listened to the presentations and afterwards came up and said that he had been mulling over some of the questions I asked, and that he thought that I might be right. He said that we should talk. I was delighted, and asked: "When?" He responded: "Now." So he and I spent the next three days holed up in a Chicago hotel room, arguing technical points about our anti-inflation plans, and talking about economics in general.

At the end of the three days I had convinced him that my value-added price control approach was more general than his wage control approach, and that I had thought of a number of issues and nuances of the idea that he had not. His openness and total commitment to understanding was both unexpected and delightful. We could talk about highly abstract ideas that didn't have formal models. He suggested we should do a book together, spelling out the ideas we had discussed. I asked: "When?" He said: "Next Month." So that December I flew from Europe, where I was a research fellow at Oxford, to Tallahassee, where Abba was teaching, to work on the book. There, I rose at 6 a.m. every morning, and we worked until 9 p.m. I'd write a draft; Abba would rework it, and we'd continue working like that throughout the day. Although Abba was in his 70s then, he still lived and breathed economics. At the end of December, a draft of an article and of the book was complete.

Abba and I got along fantastically; our views of economics were almost identical. We differed primarily in two ways: First, Abba was an unabashed utilitarian, and I was not. Second, while he was much more interested in the idea as a practical policy than I was, he was amazingly naive about politics. I was far more politically aware than he: he felt good ideas rose because they were good; I, at that point, was far more jaundiced, and felt that everything happens because it is in the relevant people's interest, and good ideas are often not in the relevant people's interest.

We were, however, quite different in temperament. Abba was the perfectionist who would work over every word and phrase; I was interested in the grand conception—the specifics were simply a boring job that had to be done. This difference in temperament made the collaboration even more fruitful, and it was a delight working with him. (His wife Daliah made it even more of a delight; she put up with us and made the technicalities of life disappear.)

In writing jointly with someone, one of the two must have final say, and given our different positions, it was clear that Abba would have final say. This presented no problem on most issues, since we agreed, but there was one area of disagreement where our conception of what we called MAP (the market anti-inflation plan) differed, even after long discussion. Abba saw our market anti-inflation plan as simply a way to control the price level, and argued that when imposed, the price of changing price would quickly go to zero, since all people would be doing would be setting relative prices. I argued for a quite different conception in which the nominal and real sectors were intertwined and where, depending on aggregate demand pressure, there would be a different equilibrium level of output with each different equilibrium price of raising price. Abba saw a knife-edge equilibrium, except for frictions; I saw a multitude of equilibria and the likelihood that given existing institutions the aggregate equilibrium the economy reached was an excess supply equilibrium.

This was a major theoretical difference. My interpretation required a radical rethinking of macro theory since it meant that the nominal price-setting institutions influenced real economic variables in a systematic way. His interpretation saw MAP as fitting in nicely with existing macro theory—simply a way to control the price level.

In our joint work we followed Abba's conception; in my individual work I spelled out my conception and we continually discussed the differences when we were together. The last serious discussion we had about it was in England in 1980 where we were attending a conference on TIP. That evening we sat around arguing and I related the idea back to Abba's seminal 1934 article on degrees of monopoly. It was as if a light bulb went off in his head, and he finally tentatively agreed with me. We agreed to discuss it more when he returned from Israel, which was the next leg of his journey. Unfortunately he had a stroke in Israel that impaired his language ability, and we never had that conversation. Happily, he remained physically well after his stroke, but we never again could work together. We remained close friends until his death in 1982.

The importance of Abba to my career as an economist is inestimable. It is entirely possible that I would have left the profession had not Abba picked me up, encouraged me, and made it possible for me to publish. The reception accorded to our joint work was fundamentally different than the reception my solo work got; it was considered; people actually talked about the idea, even though it didn't flow from a formal model. The reason was that Abba was known as the generator of odd schemes, and was also seen as an icon from the past. But Abba was also known for being quite impractical and far out, so the idea was not taken seriously. But at least it was discussed, and it made a nice follow-up to discussions of TIPs—it was the market equivalent to TIPs, just as marketable permits for pollution are the market equivalent to pollution taxes.

Abba's whole life was economics, and he would take me around with him to the inner-circle cocktail parties where the insiders of the profession meet and informally talk economics. It is here where the old-timers meet the newcomers. Abba would introduce me to people, and say very nice things about me. Sometimes that introduction would cause people to remember my name, and treat me a bit differently from other neophytes. I became known as Abba's protégé and many thought that I had been his student. Put simply, Abba made it possible for me to exist in the economics profession.

But while Abba had access to the inner circle, Abba was not an inner-circle economist; he never was; instead, he was a tangential iconoclast who in his old age was adopted by the profession much more than he was when he was young.

In many ways Abba was a bit of an embarrassment to the inner circle of the profession in that he continued to come up with politically hopeless schemes to improve the efficiency of the economy. It was rumored that Abba was on the short list for the Nobel Prize—I suspect our work on MAP played a role in his not getting the Prize, since MAP was far too controversial, and he would likely have used the Nobel speech as a podium for telling people about it, and claiming it was the solution to society's ills. That is not what I suspect the inner circle would have wanted from a Nobel Prize winner. Thus, Abba's high regard for me was both a blessing and a curse since, if Abba liked me, I, too, must be a tangential iconoclast. It was a curse I could live with.

My association with Abba catapulted me from struggling outsider to a small-time, known, but somewhat strange, gadfly economist. Being so known within some circles meant that I could get published reasonably easily within a restricted range of journals. It also led to my being offered an endowed distinguished chair at Middlebury College, which I accepted. I have enjoyed teaching there immensely.

Abba and I worked together for only four years; he had his stroke and I was on my own again. But life after Abba was quite different from life before Abba. The chair gave me some influence and respect, as well as a small budget to run conferences. At these conferences I tried to bring economists of different persuasions together and to look at issues from a slightly different perspective. They focused on ideas, not models. Those conferences, and the volumes I edited based on them, gave me a chance to meet, and carry on, the acquaintances I had made while with Abba, and to develop an independent reputation as a non-partisan heterodox economist.

The move to Middlebury also helped change my research agenda—from one focusing on abstract theory to one focusing on teaching and methodology. The reasons for this change were twofold. First, when I came to Middlebury, I tried to teach an upper-level course on the micro foundations of macro; I had three students sign up, two of whom were totally mathematically unprepared. Moreover, the passion of the one who was mathematically prepared was for music, not math. She has since become a professional harpsichordist. It was clear to me that if I were going to keep an active research agenda and be a good teacher, these two areas of my life must be combined. So I began concentrating more on what I call "the translation problem"—reducing the high-level theory to teachable models that convey the essence of the high-level theory.

As I studied this issue I became convinced that, as a profession, we were doing a horrendous job in that translation, and that the models we taught to undergraduates were not the models we believed, and that the empirical work we were doing and teaching students was not the way we convinced ourselves of the validity of propositions. The recognition of this conflict led to my work on the profession, which has been far better received by the profession than my theoretical work has been.

As I was doing this work on models I discovered that I had a knack for textbooks. Textbooks gave me a wider forum for my ideas, and were profitable. I have come to believe that what goes into textbooks probably plays a more important role in the future direction of the profession than just about anything else economists do. Textbooks' tone and the vision they convey play an important role in selecting who chooses to continue studying economics, and what vision they carry with them. It is in textbooks that the foundation of the future of economic research is laid.

With each successful book and article more offers to write come in, and I am now at the stage of my career where I am having to learn to say "no" to invitations to write and speak. I am learning to do this in an attempt to maintain my sanity and my creativity. The reason I say the latter is that there is a perverse connection between the requests one gets to write and how well known one's views on a subject are. The better known one's views, the more requests to express them one gets. So I am now trying to follow the philosophy of turning down most request to write on the profession where my views are relatively well known among economists, and am concentrating on areas where my views aren't well known, and where I will likely get rejected. My latest work on the macrofoundations of micro falls within this classification. That work, however, meets my Yeah criterion, so I will predict that within ten years some variation of it will be all the rage in macro. When I've had my say there, I will then turn my attention to the cost problem and to showing the profession that Jacob Viner's intuition was right after all.

NOTES

*   I would like to thank Harry Landreth, Michael Szenberg, and Tom Mayer for helpful comments on earlier drafts.

1.   When he read this essay, Tom Mayer pointed out to me that the Yeah criterion is similar to Fritz Machlup's "aha-ness." I suspect that it appears under other names for other intuitively-oriented economists and scientists.

2.   For those who do not know of Viner's mistake, it was telling the draftsman to draw the short-run marginal cost curves through the minimum point of the short-run average costs curves and to simultaneously draw them through the point where the short-run cost curve is tangent to the long-run average cost curve. Scholar that he is, Viner left the mistake for all to see, along with his admission that it was a mistake, when his famous article that set up the standard cost analysis was reprinted. See Jacob Viner (1931).

3.   J.B. Clark's relating of marginal product and justice is an example of the type of problem that existed. Obviously not all non-mathematical intuitive economists have believed that markets solve all problems. For example, in the early 1900s institutionalism was strong. But by the 1920s the more doctrinaire laissez faire economists were an important part of the inner circle of the profession.

4.   I often try to conceptualize fundamentally different systems as a way of gaining insight into a current system; thus I have worked through in my mind multiple goods-monies economies, economies in which all consumption is joint and all production is individual, and economies in which production, not consumption, is the goal.

8.   Surviving as a Slightly Out of Sync Economist

I have survived reasonably well in the profession, even though I have followed my own path, at least to some degree. That, I suspect, is the reason I was asked to contribute to Steven Medema and Warren Samuels' book, *Foundations of Research in Economics: How Do Economists Do Economics*.

One of the ways in which I differ from most economists is in the way I believe institutions should be integrated into economic thinking. I see institutions as central to our understanding of the economy. One cannot understand the economy unless one understands the way institutions work. Most mainstream economists tend to see institutions as a type of friction—institutions may slow down the workings of economic forces, but otherwise they play no role. Consistent with that view graduate economics students are taught that markets work, and that one can understand how to operate within markets without understanding real-world institutions. Many students actually believe what they are taught.

That belief leads to problems for many students since the economics profession, like any other profession, has its institutional realities, and if one is to succeed in the profession, or even simply stay in it, one must understand those institutional realities and learn to operate within them. Given the mainstream view of institutions, it isn't surprising that many, otherwise bright, students never learn to cope with those institutional realities. After graduate school, students are thrown out into the real world, and they either learn about the institutional realities of our profession quickly, or they leave the profession.[1]

Let me give some examples. Recently a young assistant professor—five years out of graduate school—was attempting to apply to other, higher-level, universities for a full-time position. He believed that since he had a strong publishing record, and was a good teacher, he would do well in his search. He quickly discovered that in the economics profession internal labor markets are alive and well. A career path moving from a lower- to higher-level school after five years is institutionally discouraged. Another example came when I was in a late night discussion with some young economists after a conference. A couple of these young economists actually believed that the stated rules of tenure were the actual rules used! Imagine! I quickly dissuaded them from such naive beliefs.

108

Where one learns about institutional realities is in late-night, informal discussions with older economists. In these conversations, the older economists take down their guards and tell younger economists how the economics profession really works. Unfortunately, many graduate students and young assistant professors have not spent enough time in bars. Hence this essay. It is a modified transcript of such a late night discussion in a bar.

A LATE-NIGHT CONVERSATION

The Setting: A hotel lounge at about 11:00 p.m. after an economics conference. I'm there with a scotch; a few young assistant professors are sitting there with me.

"OK, Colander," one of them says. "You're the great moralizer; how should economics be done?"

"My first piece of advice is my standard warning about advice: listen to that advice, but don't necessarily follow it."

Having absolved myself from the guilt that I would feel if someone actually followed my advice, I get down to the real nitty-gritty advice.

"My next piece of advice on how to do economics is to first decide what you think economics should be, and what you see as your role in furthering that view of economics. You must make that decision before you can make a reasonable decision about how to do economics. While that advice may sound trite, I suspect that few young economists have articulated to themselves what they think economics should be, and whether it is what it should be. And fewer still have thought about what their role in furthering their conception of economics is. Yet their answer to those questions makes a fundamental difference as to how they should do economics. Trite advice is not always stupid advice."

"OK, enough qualifying—we're all young professors at liberal arts schools who are sitting with you, so, obviously, we're sympathetic with your view of economics. So for us, how should we do economics?"

"As I said, my advice on how to do economics is dependent on what one believes economics should be. So let me explain my view."

HOW, IDEALLY, ECONOMICS SHOULD BE DONE

In my view, the primary reason society gives money to academic economists (those of them who are not being supported by research grants) is for teaching. And that money is primarily for teaching principles of economics, which, in my mind, centers around teaching economic reasoning. Doing economics well therefore means doing well the job we are paid for; it means teaching economic reasoning to society.

In emphasizing teaching as what economists should do, I know I am going against the grain of many economists (non-mainstream as well as mainstream), who often, in conversation, denigrate teaching and exalt research—especially research extending the frontiers of economic knowledge. I find it perverse, and morally wrong, to denigrate teaching, and, as the profession has done, to design institutions to channel money surreptitiously away from teaching and into "research," justifying those actions by some inherent "goodness" of basic research that politicians don't understand. In my view the research that should get most weight in universities and colleges is research that is derivative of teaching, not the other way around. Thus, much of my thinking about economics concerns the teaching of economics—how we can translate the highest level ideas on economic issues into understandable examples for students.

I even have some rules of good teaching. They are:

1. Consider teaching important. Spend lots of time preparing. Make your lectures fun. Make them exciting. Don't repeat what's in the book; go beyond it. Excite the student about the ideas.
2. Do not let the medium become the message. Teach economics, not techniques.
3. Spend time with your students. Read broadly and carry the knowledge of that reading into class. Talk the students' language.
4. Teach with passion, or don't teach. Life is too short, and economics too much fun.
5. Use examples that relate to your students. Relate economic reasoning to their life.
6. Distinguish among various types of models. Use technical modeling as a method of exercising students' minds; do not apply the models when they really don't apply.
7. Listen to others' advice on teaching, but don't necessarily follow anyone else's rules of teaching. Each person is unique.

THE ROLE OF RESEARCH IN GOOD TEACHING

Since teaching is primary, one might think that I put little store in research. Such a belief would be wrong for two reasons. The first is that I like abstract research. That's the reason I was initially attracted to economics—I got paid to play all these fun games that had no relevance at all to anything. I still enjoy putting my two cents in when playing with those puzzles. However, after I had been playing the game of economics for a while, it lost some of its enjoyment for me, and it seemed to be getting further and further removed from reality. I started to look at the economics profession from society's point of view. That's when I wrote the *Garbagemen* book (Colander, 1991).

Essentially, I became convinced that the economics profession was extracting rents from society, and not producing enough of the services society wants and needs—teaching economic reasoning. All this is not to say that abstract research has no role. But it is not the aspect of economics that, I believe, society most values, nor is it the type of research that I believe should get high rankings in tenure reviews in liberal arts schools, nor for that matter in graduate schools.[2] While playing the economics puzzle game sharpens one's economic intuition, it often becomes an end in itself, drawing one away from teaching in the same way that a passion for playing bridge draws one away from teaching economics. If one gets grants to do such puzzle research, fine, but if you're paid to be a professor, your academic focus should be on teaching.

The second reason I place enormous importance on research is that there is another type of research that is extremely relevant to professors at liberal arts schools. It is what I call teaching-relevant research. By teaching-relevant research I mean research that reflects the type of skills we want our students to have once they graduate—an ability to express insightful, economic ideas well in language that is understandable and persuasive. Teaching-relevant research involves clear, concise writing. Teaching-relevant research conveys a deep understanding of economic principles in simple terms. It is research that shows institutional understanding, a knowledge of economic theory, and a sense of judgment. I favor this type of research because it directly complements teaching, rather than pulling one away from teaching, as much puzzle-solving research does.

I even have some rules of good teaching-relevant research. They are:

1. Ask meaningful questions; someone besides a small number of economists should be interested in the results of your research, and you should be able to explain to a lay person why your research is of interest.
2. Ask manageable questions. By that I mean asking questions that can be dealt with using data you have available for research and choosing a research question with which you have sufficient time to deal.
3. Use a research technique and mode of expression with which you are comfortable. Otherwise the technique overwhelms the analysis and you lose judgment.
4. Know previous research done on the subject—and be able to explain how your research fits in. You should expand, not duplicate, previous work.

5. If you use econometrics, you should be familiar with the methods of collecting data, and with the institutions from which that data is drawn.
6. Do not be falsely scientific.
7. Carefully consider the question of your research from all sides.
8. Do not violate the law of significant digits. Be no more precise than the least precise dimension of the question you are considering.

If professors can't do teaching-relevant research, and do it well, then there is a question whether they are comfortable in their writing and in their knowledge of the subject, which would lead me to question whether they will be good teachers. Being a good teacher is not necessarily being liked by the students—a good teacher conveys understanding and skills to students rather than simply entertaining them. If a professor doesn't have the understanding of economics and the skills to undertake teaching-relevant research, he or she will have a hard time being a good teacher.

Let me give examples of what I consider relevant and irrelevant research for teaching purposes.[3]

Non-teaching-relevant research

*   Designing a formal model to determine whether fixed or flexible exchange rates are preferable. Reason irrelevant: Generally the data and institutional knowledge needed to have anything relevant to say on this issue is beyond a liberal arts professor, and most graduate professors.
*   Determining whether data series are stationary. Reason irrelevant: too esoteric to teach most undergraduates.
*   Designing an overlapping-generations model that requires many limiting assumptions in order to solve. Reason irrelevant: These assumptions inevitably overwhelm the model, and make the results meaningless for real-world application.

Teaching-relevant research

*   Cost-benefit analysis of a local recycling program. Reason relevant: One can collect the data and know the empirical results.
*   Determining whether an electric company's energy conservation program makes any sense. Reason relevant: This involves the simple application of economic principles to a manageable question.

Here my young colleagues say, "So what you are advising us to do is to focus on teaching and to do teaching-oriented research—right?"

INSTITUTIONAL INCENTIVES

"Wrong, wrong, wrong," I say, reaching for another scotch. "Remember what I said at the beginning. To decide how to do economics you must first decide what economics should be, but that decision is simply a preliminary decision in deciding how one should actually do economics. To decide how to do economics you must relate what you believe should be done to the institutional incentives for doing what will get you ahead. If doing economics the way you believe it should be done gets you tossed out of the profession, then it is not a good strategy for doing economics. The reality is that if you want to survive, you have to do economics in a way that satisfies institutional constraints. If you don't, you won't survive as an economist. This is why you must understand the nature of the institution and the decision-making process within that institution. Real-world rationality is institutionally specific; to think too globally in a world characterized by overlapping institutions is a sure path to failure."

A successful person is one who understands the incentives in the system sufficiently so that he or she can exist within the system, but who simultaneously maintains a broader sense of what he or she believes is important. This melding, in my view, is fundamental to one's psychic, and to one's institutional, well-being.

Put in economic jargon, life is a constrained, not a global, optimization problem. For economists who believe that existing institutional incentives are for good economics, this presents no problem. But for economists like me, who believe existing institutions include many perverse incentives, it presents a serious problem. Let me spell out what I believe are some of the existing incentives, and then relate those incentives to the reality of the job market and advancement process that all young economists face.

The real-world institutional incentives are not for doing teaching-relevant research; they are for writing game-playing articles. Design a model, solve it, and publish it. Don't worry that these formal models have little real relevance to the ongoing policy debates, or to the designers' teaching. For empirical work the incentives are to get some data and run some formal econometric tests on that data without really understanding the institutions that generated the data, and to publish it as supposedly meaning something. The incentives are to spend little time really teaching students, and to entertain them in the time you do spend teaching, so that you get good evaluations. The incentives are to spend time teaching modeling techniques, not economic reasoning. So for me, there is a difference between what economists do, and what economists should do.

FINDING AN ACCEPTABLE COMPROMISE

If one agrees with me about these differences, the real question is to what degree one should do 'good work' and to what degree one must do work that the institutional structure rewards. As I have gone around and talked to graduate students and young professors, I am continually amazed by the naiveté of many of them; they think of the economics profession as pure academic pursuit in which the search for the truth will be rewarded, quality work will overwhelm non-quality work, and people will be judged on the merits of their teaching and research. To that I say hogwash. While there are certain tendencies for good work to succeed, these tendencies are weak and often are thwarted by other tendencies built into the institutional structure of economics.[4]

My recommendation to a young professor is not: "Do what you believe economics should be; the world will recognize quality." That just isn't true. Instead, one should recognize that existing economists do what they do because there are institutional incentives to do it. One focuses on one's conception of what one should do (if it is different from the institution's conception) only at a cost, and it is a cost that is larger than many young economists can bear. For most economists it is necessary to compromise, with the degree of compromise determined by their opportunity cost. By that I mean that if one's psyche needs social reinforcement, or if one has responsibility for feeding a family of four and no money stashed in a trust fund, the optimal strategy is quite different than if one is a psychologically secure, egotistical heir to a large fortune. I direct my moralistic preaching about what economics should be, and how I believe economics should be done, at tenured insiders who make the decisions about tenure, and at journal editors who decide what to publish.

INSTITUTIONAL REALITIES OF THE ECONOMICS PROFESSION

The compromise that one will be required to make depends on the institution where one is. Economics is not a homogeneous field (although it is more homogeneous than I believe it should be), and thus institutional realities differ. Despite the differences, I will try to list some generic institutional realities that I believe exist. I'll deal with the three issues that are central to surviving as an academic economist: finding a job, keeping a job, and publishing. At that point I will stop since once one has made it that far, one should be aware of the institutional realities, and be at a level to change them, or to pass on the information to others.

The Realities of the Economic Job Market

The economics job market, like any other job market, has its own characteristics. A few of the most relevant ones for graduate students are:

1. Hiring is often done on the basis of credentials, not real qualifications. The higher ranked one's graduate school, the more probable one will get an offer from a high-level school.
2. Recommendations from important people are extremely important. Top-level university campus interviews are almost always based on personal calls from one's advisor saying So-and-So is a hot prospect. There are few walk-ons in economics. Also, it is important to recognize that all letters of recommendation are positive; even a slight negative can hurt significantly if you are in the general pool of applicants.
3. Informal contacts—and phone calls by your advisors and friends—are important for getting considered for jobs.
4. After you are considered for a job, the most important determinant of getting a job is the impression you make on the decision makers. It helps enormously to know their research and know their approaches before you go to present a paper.
5. The general state of the job market in particular fields plays a big role in your chances of being hired in the general market.
6. Job markets are internal to schools; there exists much more flexibility for new hires than for lateral moves (changing schools after a few years). Thus, it is important to choose a school initially with which one is compatible.
7. Individuals on temporary appointments who meet the schools' qualifications often have an inside track for tenure-track jobs, should such a job come up. However, temporary jobs focusing on teaching at a research-oriented university are inevitably dead-end jobs.
8. If you leave a school after a period of time, you will most likely move to a lower-ranked school. If you have moved around significantly early on, it is harder to land a job than if you are just entering the market from graduate school.

Because of the internal nature of the job market, the initial choice of school is highly important to your success. It should be chosen with specific knowledge of what the school's actual teaching and research expectations are. If you want to do economics your way, and that differs from the mainstream's way, take the job at a school where people are open to your approach, not the job at the highest–ranked school that offers you one.

The Realities of Keeping a Job

Generally, the rules of tenure at a school are not the stated ones. In your initial discussion with those schools it's important to find out what the actual rules for tenure are. While it is, again, difficult to generalize, I will try.

1.   Often teaching receives much lower ranking in the advancement criteria than does research. The stated rules often include an even split among teaching, service, and research; the actual rules are often 75 per cent research, 20 per cent being friendly with the right people, 5 per cent teaching.
2.   Research seldom means teaching-relevant -research. Research means publishing in the "right" journals. "Right" journals differ among schools, but the general rule is the higher the ranking of the journal in some ranking, the "righter" it is likely to be. (That's why there are so many alternative rankings; one can choose the ranking that serves one's purpose.)
3.   Decisions of acceptable research are often quantitative, not qualitative. While only a few schools will come out and say it, research requirements are often "x number of ranked-weighted articles." Thus my advice to young economists has been always carefully to consider one's research strategy and combine it with a realistic publication strategy that meets the institutional goals of the school where one is teaching. If one has an unpleasant personality, one should significantly exceed the institution's goals. If one's background and interest don't mesh with a school, don't take a job there; the odds are too heavily stacked against one.
4.   Total immersion in your research early on is almost a necessity. The reason is that from the time of conception of an idea until publication is often a multi-year process. If you do not start early, you'll likely never catch up. Tenure committees have seen much work in progress, and, if they like you, they will give work in progress some weight, but if they don't, they won't. Actual acceptances are much stronger than "work in progress."
5.   Don't be too obvious about structuring your research to fit decision maker's views of what good research is. Seem to have some gumption even if you have none. Understand, but do not blatantly play up to, biases of decision makers. Everyone knows the game, but often it isn't really talked about. Subtlety is admired in academia.

Because the journal ranking is so important, and is school-specific, it is critical to find out what the journal ranking is that decision makers use, and to concentrate your publishing on that school's highly-ranked journals. You should check with the decision makers—preferably informally—about what the right journals are and choose a school where their right journals most closely match yours. Frank discussion about such issues early on is necessary for you to structure your research agenda accordingly. I'm at a liberal arts school because most of my right journals have a different philosophy about what economics should be than do journals that most universities think are right. Whatever the case, be prepared to structure your research to fit your school's "right journals," at least until after tenure; you are not going to change the system if you don't get tenure.

The Realities of Publishing

How does one publish in these "right" journals, you ask? You don't do it by reading an article, getting an idea from that article, and working two years on your article. The reason is that what's published is generally last year's interest; it will likely not be next year's interest when you are ready to send your paper in. Publication of a journal article is in many ways a tombstone to an economic debate, not an opening of it.

In thinking about publishing in a journal it is important to recognize that journals have their own institutional and sociological structures. The debates that show up in the journals are often ones that have been carried on at academic meetings, or in workshops, or at bars, three or four years earlier. Unless you are part of those early meetings, or you, in some way, understand the type of issues the editors believe important, it is difficult, if not almost impossible, to get published in that journal, regardless of the quality of your work. The obvious, interesting, questions flowing from published research will already have been mined by insiders. Occasionally one will find an untapped vein, but such a find will be an exception, not the rule.

The above arguments do not mean that publishing in these journals is impossible—it only means that to have a good chance of succeeding, it helps to be tied in. That means talking to people who are publishing there, and using the same methodology and approach as they use. A journal is a conversation and has a certain approach. Any submission to it should be made with an understanding of that approach, and if your paper deviates from it, the paper should carefully explain why it deviates. If you don't read a journal regularly, it's unlikely you'll be published in it.

How does one become part of a journal's conversation? If there's a graduate school nearby, attend workshops and seminars; often papers given at these are designed for journals. Subscribe to various Working Paper series. Attend conferences, especially specialized ones, and sit in on sessions, or, better yet, organize sessions of those economists who are working on the same area as you at regional meetings, where it is relatively easy to organize a session, or in non-AEA organized sessions of the national meetings, where you have a good chance of being allowed to do so. Doing a joint paper with someone tied into the conversation is another way of joining a conversation.

CONCLUSION

The ideas in this short "how to" guide to a young economist can be briefly summarized in four points:

1. Decide what good economics is: take that as your ultimate goal, but make the search for that goal constrained by the institutional environment. Initially, work on what the current institutional environment tells you to work on, at least enough to succeed in that institutional environment. To the degree that you have time, work on ideas that the current institutional environment does not value, but treat that work as a luxury, not as your primary research.
2. Decide what the determinants of success are in the current institutional structure. Become successful, doing what you are supposed to do, while following up in your spare time on what you believe is important.
3. After having become successful in the current institutional environment, you will have rents to spend. At that point remember your earlier idealistic beliefs about what good economics is, and spend some portion of your rents on achieving it. This will probably cost you institutionally, at least in the short run, but it will also offer the chance to connect with one's youthful idealism, which is infinitely rewarding.
4. Work toward changing institutional incentives to make it possible for other younger economists to follow what you regard as good economics. Use your energy, resources, and efforts to help such individuals advance. A well-timed positive comment can make an enormous difference to a young economist. The effect that any one individual can have on a system is small. The effect through students will dwarf the effect you can have through your writing.

Advances in a field are made by individuals who understand the system and are successful within the system, but who also do not get so sucked up into the system that they give up broader questioning of the system. It is easy to get caught up in the existing institution. Many of my graduate school colleagues started from a far more non-mainstream position than I did, but they ended up much more mainstream. The system either trivializes or transforms non-mainstream economists who do not understand and accept the system, or, if it can't do either, it eliminates those economists from the profession.

Most of us forget the passage of time—that life needs will differ, and life styles that are quite acceptable as graduate students and independent individuals are no longer acceptable once various real or illusionary responsibilities are placed upon us as we grow older. Real-world contingencies force us to accept the current institutional structure.

I'm in favor of changing the nature of the profession but I recognize that change is seldom brought about from outside; it is brought about from inside—by individuals who understand the absolute need of an imperfect institutional structure, but who also believe that it is worth working toward institutional reform even if there are few explicit rewards in working for that, and such work may even have significant costs. Only individuals willing to spend their rents on change can bring that change about, and only individuals who are successful in the current institutional structure will have rents to spend on change.

NOTES

1. Although students in most non-mainstream programs are taught that institutions are theoretically important, they are taught little about the way the economic institutions work.
2. For development of these ideas see Colander and Brenner (1992).
3. There are, of course, exceptions. Some polymath economists can do everything. They can write about abstract game theory, and teach institutionally-specific Fed policy, drawing from that research, for example. All the better. But most of us must specialize and there is a gross substitution relationship, rather than a complementarity, between high-level puzzle research and teaching undergraduates.
4. Economics is not unique among academic subjects and institutions in discouraging good work. All real-world institutions have perverse incentives; the degree to which they do, however, is institutionally specific.

PART V

Implications of the Lost Art of Economics for the Profession

9. Vision, Judgment, and Disagreement among Economists

It is often said that if you laid all the economists end to end, they still wouldn't reach an agreement. The implication of that and similar statements about economists is that there is too much disagreement among economists. I disagree; in my view, given the nature of the questions economists ask, significant disagreement is both to be expected and desirable.

Unfortunately, while I believe that the total amount of disagreement may be approximately the right amount, I also believe that the areas and reasons for disagreeing are often wrong. In my view, we often disagree about the things we should agree about, and agree about things we should disagree about.

For example, on the one hand, economists generally agree to use a mainstream model that, in my, and in many economists', view (even those who use it), does not relate to the real world, and embodies innumerable *ad hoc* assumptions. Here is an example in which more disagreement would seem warranted. On the other hand, economists spend enormous amounts of time disagreeing about what I consider relatively minor modeling issues—such as whether the Pigou effect logically exists, or the shape of the LM curve. I consider these relatively minor issues because the answers to them do not make a large difference to our policy advice.

The different models that economists use, and the different policies that economists recommend, are not dependent on minor modeling issues; they are dependent on differences in vision of how an economy operates, and in differences in judgments about how the political system would implement a policy, or on what effect the policy will have on existing institutions. But most economists' debate concerns minor issues of modeling. It is as if economists use disagreements about minor modeling issues to mask differences in vision and judgments about the dimensions of economic problems that cannot be precisely quantified.

ARTIPHOBIA

This fear of discussing differences in judgment and vision can be called artiphobia. Economists have a fear of being considered artists, who use judgment and vision to come to a conclusion, rather than being considered scientists. Artiphobia shows up in many ways. One recent example is a "slam sheet" on my introductory textbook prepared by a competing textbook author.[1] One of the major reasons why this competing author believed people should not use my book is that "Colander takes a whimsical approach to principles. In his view economics is more art than science."

Similar views of my treatment of J.N. Keynes' tripartite art/positive economics/normative economics distinction have been conveyed to me by economists who share my view that many of the differences among economists concern differences in judgment and vision, and not differences that can be captured in formal models. But they object to, or at least strongly discourage me from, using the term "art" to capture that judgment and vision aspect of economics. They believe, probably correctly, that for me to tell economists that much of what they do is art will insure that my views will not be taken seriously. Actually, I have no problem with dropping the term art; labels are unimportant. I mention the reaction my treatment provokes because it helps explain the perverse nature of economists' disagreement; our disagreements are generally on matters of judgment about the relevance of models, not technical issues within those models. But such disagreements are not allowed to be expressed explicitly since they might be considered artistic disagreements. Instead, the disagreements get reflected in disagreements about models—disagreements that "obviously" fall in science.

THE NEED FOR VISION AND JUDGMENT IN SELECTING AMONG *AD HOC* ASSUMPTIONS

To see what I mean about the importance of differences in vision in determining a theory, consider the economic problem in its full complexity: You have six billion people—all pursuing ends that are partially endogenously determined—interacting in a variety of institutional settings, using a large variety of differentiated inputs and ever-changing technologies—to arrive at some undetermined output. What will be the nature of that interaction, and what output will it lead to?

Faced with the problem of designing a core model of the aggregate economy to capture that interaction, imagine someone put the following propositions:

1. That we forget about the multitude of inputs, and use a model with only two—capital, a fixed input, and labor, a variable input.
2. That we assume away technological complexities leading to infinitely varied adjustment costs and focus only on diminishing marginal returns.

3. That we use a representative agent approach to analyzing aggregate phenomena, eliminating questions of strategic interdependence.
4. That we talk about money as a fixed concept, even though we're not sure which of the constantly changing empirical measures of money to use.
5. That we assume, for the sake of analytic convenience, that tastes are exogenous.
6. That, again for the sake of analytic convenience, we assume a simple utilitarian psychological basis for our analysis of individual decision making.
7. That when talking about the aggregate economy we aggregate up millions of different goods into an aggregate output concept, and that we can assume technical efficiency of the aggregate production function.
8. That we assume costs of rationality are zero, and people can make rational decisions intertemporally and across the full domain of goods.
9. That we can assume a unique aggregate equilibrium.

I could continue with this list, but the one I have just given should be sufficient to make my point. Given the complexity of the problem to be solved, disagreement, in the sense of diversity of research programs, should be expected.[2] That isn't what one sees. While there are small pockets of non-mainstream critics—such as Institutionalists, Post Keynesians, Austrians, and Radicals—the large majority of the profession makes up an almost hegemonic research program in which most researchers accept the broad outlines of assumptions, and then modify one or another slightly or ask questions that can be structured within the standard model.

I believe the reason we don't see major disagreements is that such disagreements would involve differences in vision and judgment. The guiding light in choosing among assumptions cannot be pure logic—the decisions are too complicated for formal logic. Instead one must rely on vision to choose that combination of simplification and admission of complexity—the *ad hoc* assumptions—that produces a model that leads to relevant insights, and that is convincing to others. Yet there is almost no discussion of disagreement about economists' vision.

The evolution of the Keynesian revolution is a case in point. There were many ways in which the Keynesian challenge to neoclassical economics could have been structured; it could have been seen as a vision fundamentally different from the Classical vision—one involving multiple aggregate equilibria, strategic interdependence, and dynamic path dependency. The way it was actually structured was within a unique aggregate equilibrium framework in which the only difference between Keynesian and Classical was a fixed nominal wage assumption. This meant that Keynesian economics was simply a special case of the Classical model. All the disagreements between Keynesians and Classicals were forced into this fixed wage framework, and thereby many of the issues raised by the Keynesian revolution were trivialized. Why? Because structuring the question this way made it fit a relatively simple model, whereas other frameworks raised far more fundamental questions.

THE NEED FOR JUDGMENT IN CHOOSING AMONG POLICIES

The policy debates, similarly, involve disagreements on issues that are not central to the reasons the profession disagrees. In policy, the true debate generally relates to judgments about non-quantifiable effects. Yet economists' debate about policy is generally formulated in terms of applied models and empirical specification. For example, we see that most economists' discussion of economic policy focuses on efficiency and on quantifying "efficiency." But efficiency is not an end in itself; it is not even a meaningful concept except as a description of achieving some other goal. The implicit assumption used in economics is that more consumption—higher standards of living— makes people happier, with little discussion of how that "more consumption" leads people to be happier, or what problems more consumption might involve, or whether the process of fulfilling desires creates further desires.

Let me give a specific example. One of the most powerful economic policy arguments I have seen lately is made by Charles Murray. Murray, who is not an economist, used standard economic arguments to argue that public welfare is bad for people because it destroys the social fabric of society. He reasoned that, given current US institutions, because people do not have to face the consequences of their actions—having to feed their children, for example— the number of unwed mothers has increased significantly, and will continue to increase. Eventually, he argued, the institution of the family will be destroyed. Many economists agree in part with Murray's argument, but discussions about the effect of public welfare on the structure of the family have not filled the economists' journals because the argument cannot be quantified and placed in a formal model. How does one specify the "efficiency" of the family? More generally, institutions cannot be easily modeled, so they are typically left out of economists' models.

Resolving questions about assumptions and on differences in judgment has little to do with formal empirical tests as economists usually conduct them. As Thomas Mayer (1993b) and Edward Leamer (1978, 1983) have convincingly argued, given the nature of observation in economics, empirical tests at this level are inevitably indecisive. Numerous theories and judgments can be interpreted as consistent with the data.

One example of the way in which statistics are used can be seen in Martin Feldstein's 1974 study of the effect of the social security system on savings rates. He published the study in a major economics journal, providing empirical support for his position that the existence of an unfunded social security system in the United States was significantly decreasing the savings rate. Two researchers (Leimer and Selig, 1982) tried to replicate his study, but could not. It was found that a data input error had led to Feldstein's result, and that, when that error was corrected, his model showed that the unfunded social security system had a positive, not a negative, effect on the savings rate! Did this result cause Feldstein to change his policy proposals? No. Instead he redid his empirical study, adjusting the model, and came out with a slight negative effect of the unfunded system on the savings rate.

The point of this example is not that a data input mistake was made, although as Dewald *et al.* (1986) have shown, such mistakes happen relatively often. The point is the way in which "empirical evidence" is used. To structure a model that will capture the effect of social security on the savings rate, enormous *ad hoc* assumptions must be made to develop the data. These *ad hoc* assumptions make it impossible for the empirical analysis to be definitive. Feldstein knew that, and he, correctly, did not change his policy position when the data input error was found. His policy position was based on a much broader combination of vision and judgment. But in the study he did not make his argument based on that vision and judgment; instead he translated a position based on judgment into formal empirical evidence that looked scientific and definitive, but was not and could not be.

Admitting that most policy conclusions are arrived at by a combination of judgment, vision, formal and informal empirical evidence, and a knowledge of history and institutions has a cost; it raises what might be called the "expert question." Why should policymakers, or anyone, rely on economists' judgment rather than someone else's? I believe the answer to this question should be the following: One should rely on economists' judgment because they have studied the history and the institutions and have training in interpreting the empirical evidence. This training in judgment makes them better qualified than most other people to offer advice on policy, and, when one understands the economists' reasoning, it will be more convincing than other people's reasoning. That's the answer that should be given. The answer to which the current structure of the profession directs economists is that the mantle of science legitimizes economists' policy pronouncements. Instead of admitting that policy decisions must be made on informed judgment, and that judgment is best left to experts, the economics profession has chosen to look impressive, and to try to "snow" policymakers.

INSTITUTIONS, ECONOMISTS, AND DISAGREEMENT

Economists are not born with artiphobia; it is bred into them through selection mechanisms, limiting who becomes an economist and who advances as an economist, and through constant institutional reinforcement. Thus, the artiphobia explanation of the perverse nature of economists' disagreement is only a surface explanation. To explore beneath that surface and explain why this perversity of agreement exists, one must examine the incentives in the academic institutional environment within which economists operate.

I believe that institutional structure channels economists' self-interested behavior into what might be called microdisagreements—disagreements that don't really matter—and away from macrodisagreements—disagreements about core issues—that would significantly change their analysis. The reason is that the microdisagreements avoid the appearances of an art, whereas macrodisagreements would be considered directly as differences in judgment and thus would fall into what I have classified as an art.

AN ECONOMIC APPROACH TO AGREEMENT

To see my argument about how and why institutions reinforce economists' artiphobia, it is useful to consider the question of agreement and disagreement among economists within an economic framework. In this framework there are costs and benefits to agreeing and to disagreeing. Individuals weigh those costs and benefits and choose their optimal private level of disagreement. When it is in a person's interest to agree, he or she agrees, even if what he or she is agreeing about is intuitively disagreeable and far-fetched. And, when it is in a person's interest to disagree, he or she disagrees, even if the disagreement is about something relatively small. Thus the institutional structure that determines the costs and benefits of agreeing is central to an understanding of the nature of disagreement in economics.

The last round of GATT talks (in the 1990s, before the WTO took over) provides an example of this economic cost-benefit analysis of agreement and of the importance of institutional structure. These GATT talks dragged on interminably, with the same issues being discussed over and over again. They went on two years longer than planned. Why the continued disagreement? Clearly part of the reason had to do with the contentiousness of the issues involved. But the economic approach to agreement directs one to consider the incentives created by the institutional structure: What were the costs and benefits of agreeing and disagreeing?

To answer that question, consider where the talks were held: in the pleasant surroundings of Geneva over expensive meals. Given these surroundings, the benefits of disagreeing to the participants were high, and the costs were low; the economic approach suggests that the disagreement would be continued as long as possible. Had those talks taken place in Buffalo in winter (and all the excellent restaurants in Buffalo had been closed down), the GATT talks would have come to a quick resolution.

GATT, of course, was as much about political as it was about economic agreement. But the issues are the same for any economic problem, be it one of theory or of policy. People agree and disagree when it is in their interest to do so, and the institutional structure within which they operate determines their interest.[3]

The statement that agreement depends on the costs and benefits of agreeing is, like much economic analysis, logically correct, but empirically vacuous, in the sense that it simply pushes the analysis back to what determines the costs and benefits. Thus in no way am I arguing that the economic approach is sufficient. The economic approach simply provides a framework of analysis that is useful in the same way that Arabic numerals are useful: One can build an elegant, logically correct system of analysis around them that sheds more light than would an analysis built around some other number system, such as the Roman system. Similarly with economic analysis.

INCENTIVES FOR AGREEMENT AND DISAGREEMENT

What the economic approach does is to direct us to look at how institutions structure the incentives for agreement and disagreement of economists. How will agreeing or disagreeing on an issue help an economist achieve his or her goals within the institutional framework where he or she operates?

The institutional framework within which academic economists operate is one of tenure and quantitative publication requirements based upon rankings of journals. Advancement in the profession depends on publication. It follows that if a disagreement can be stated and resolved in print, it is much more valuable for the participants than if that same disagreement is settled elsewhere. For example, there is little incentive for one economist to call up another with whom he or she disagrees, and try to work out the disagreements over the phone. Thus, there is much disagreement based on misinterpretation. This interpretative disagreement could be relatively easily resolved by letter or phone or fax or e-mail, but instead it fills the pages of journals with models which are not getting at the true nature of the disagreement.

One of the most insightful pieces in economics that I have seen is Arjo Klamer's *Conversations with Economists* (1984). In that book Klamer published his interviews with various top macroeconomists, asking questions about debates New Classicals were having with Keynesians. What was amazing to me about these conversations was how little effort was made by these economists to actually specify the precise nature of their agreement and disagreement with their "opponents." Often one side's view of the arguments was quite different from another side's. Each side developed a caricature of the other side, and it debated that caricature, not the other side. The only serious interaction among these competing sides occurred in formal journal articles, and that required maintaining caricatures of each side. No serious attempt was made to resolve the differences efficiently. The economic approach to agreement explains this phenomenon; discussing the issues privately would have had reduced private benefits of disagreement.

A second way in which the academic institutional structure influences the nature of the disagreement among economists is that it focuses that disagreement on technical and formal empirical issues, and away from issues of judgment. Technical and empirical disagreements look more impressive, and can generate more "resolvable disputes." The problem with disputes in judgment and vision are that they are unresolvable in articles. Thus, self-interest channels disagreement away from disagreement of judgment and vision, and toward "resolvable disputes" about technical matters.

The publication institutions are not structured for major disagreements about assumptions—they are much more structured for definable disagreements, given the major assumptions. Such technical and empirical disputes have another advantage: Since they do not resolve the issue, they leave open the possibility of re-examining the issue again and again, creating more grist for articles leading to tenure and promotion. One of the most telling remarks ever made to me came from an extraordinarily bright, but relatively unknown, Oxford economist who combined judgment with technical expertise. When I asked him why he wasn't better known he said that it was because when he tackled a subject, he answered it to the degree it could be answered; thus, his work stopped research in a topic.

Let me give an example of the profession's proclivity to avoid fundamental disputes, an example that involves the use of macroeconometric models. Robert Basmann (1972) strongly condemned the structure and use of macroeconometrics in general, and the Brookings model in particular, arguing that it was pretending to be something that it wasn't and that it lacked a scientific basis. This was a challenge to the major assumptions. His critique was essentially ignored. Reflecting on Basmann's criticism, Lawrence Klein *et al.* (1991) again dismissed Basmann's critique, reiterating Fromm and Klein's (1972) statement that if one "took Basmann's critique seriously, inductive science must perish" (p. 79). This is one of many examples. A disagreement that cuts to the core is ignored, not because it may or may not be correct, but because the institutional structure strongly discourages such major disagreements.[3]

WHY ARTIPHOBIA DEVELOPED

The institutions that determine the incentives for agreement and disagreement are not *ad hoc*. They have developed for reasons and, if they work effectively, they should be designed to create incentives so that disagreements are optimally resolved. But there is no reason why one should expect optimal institutions to develop, and there is a strong reason why one should expect that suboptimal institutions will develop. The reasoning that supports me here is similar to the reasoning that public choice theorists use in explaining why government spending programs become too large.

The costs and benefits of developing institutions tend to reflect the needs of individuals within the institutions rather than the needs of society. The reason is that the benefits of creating institutions, while overall large, are broadly distributed and small on a societal per-person basis but are relatively large on a per-person basis for the individuals who work within those institutions. Thus, as a general rule, institutions develop that have, from society's point of view, incentives that direct people's private interest away from society's interest. This might be called The Theorem of Perverse Institutions.

Academic economic institutions are more perverse than most institutions because they were designed around a technology that did not pan out. In the 1950s it was believed that econometrics was going to provide a technological change that would transform the nature of disagreement among economists by providing definitive tests of theories. Much of the modern structure of economic argumentation and methodology that I find perverse was designed around that belief. That methodology directed researchers toward highly formal analysis—structured in a way that would be susceptible to empirical tests. Incoming economists were taught what might be called "classical econometric intuition." They were taught to replace their own intuition with a refined intuition based on econometric empirical tests. They were taught to limit arguments to those susceptible, at least in principle, to formal econometric testing, and to structure the arguments themselves in a formal way so that eventually they can be resolved by empirical testing.

Unfortunately, econometric testing has proven far less definitive than was initially hoped. Dealing with this failure has been difficult for the economics profession. The institutional incentives in the profession are to base your argumentation and analysis on this econometric testing, and not on debatable judgment and sensibility. Yet most of the issues at debate concern judgment and sensibility, and are not susceptible to formal empirical tests. The problems this creates are predictable. When industry has designed its structure around a technology, and that technology doesn't pan out, there will inevitably be serious problems.

INSTITUTIONAL SCREENING EFFECTS

Another way in which the institutional structure has played a role in structuring the nature of disagreement in the profession is in its effect on the personality of the individuals within the profession. In this world there are contentious people who will make big challenges, and there are uncontentious people who will focus their energies more narrowly. Similarly, there are people who excel in broad vision, and judgment, and those who excel in more technical areas. The screening process that selects which people go into a field, and which do not, plays a big role in determining the nature of agreement and disagreement in a profession.

Currently, the economic profession's institutional screening process channels a particular type of individual into economics, and that, I believe, is another reason why disagreements in economics take the form that they do.

Consider the following four candidates applying for a top graduate economics program:

Candidate AI: An economics major—a bright generalist. GPA: 3.9; GREs: math - 740; English - 760; two courses in calculus and one in statistics; wide range of extracurricular activities. Relatively uncontentious; he generally goes along.

Candidate A2:   An economics major— a bright generalist. GPA: 3.9; GREs: math - 740; English - 760; two courses in calculus and one in statistics; wide range of extracurricular activities. Relatively contentious; she challenges everything.

Candidate BI: A physics major. GPA: 3.9; GREs: math - 790; English - 620; minors in both mathematics and economics; seven courses in math; few extracurricular activities. Relatively uncontentious; she generally goes along.

Candidate B2:   A physics major. GPA: 3.9; GREs: math - 790; English - 620; minors in both mathematics and economics; seven courses in math; few extracurricular activities. Relatively contentious; he challenges everything.

All four of these people are what I would consider excellent candidates. A strong profession would be made up of a mix of the four types; their interaction and disagreement would strengthen the profession. Unfortunately, the current institutional structure is not hospitable to such disagreement and interaction among these four types, and there are two reasons for that. The first reason has to do with the probability of acceptance.

My reading of the current selection process used in top graduate schools is that Candidates BI and B2 have a higher chance of making it into a top graduate program and getting financial support. That, of course, depends on who is on the selection committee, and, generally, I believe that the "A" candidates can get into a top school if they have strong undergraduate faculty support. Specifically, I would suspect that with some phone calls, some strong letters of recommendation, and some luck in who is on the selection committee, both the "A" candidates could get in, and possibly could get financial support. Still, there is a bias toward "B" type candidates; they are the ones most graduate schools would prefer because they are the ones most likely to excel initially.

Let us now consider the choice from the candidates' side.

Candidates AI and A2 are most likely have a wide range of choices in business school, or in law. Their choices may narrow down to something like the following: (1) a $80,000 job on Wall Street with significant opportunities to be challenged; (2) law school without support, but with high earning expectations in the future; or (3) a Ph.D. economics program for which they may have barely obtained financial support, and in which it is almost assured that they will have an extraordinarily difficult time in their first two years. Given these opportunity costs, very few type A candidates will choose economics, and of those that do choose it, AI candidates are more likely to choose it and stay with it through the first two years than are A2 candidates.

The choices facing type B candidates will likely be quite different. They may be deciding between a graduate physics program and a graduate economics program. Of these two they will probably see the graduate physics program as the intellectually more challenging, but may be enticed by a higher level of financial support to go into economics. Type BI candidates are more likely to choose economics than are B2 types; in physics one is asking questions about the nature of matter, and the sky is no limit. The subject matter of economics is tame relative to the subject matter of physics.

A few type A2 and B2 candidates who choose economics programs will get their Ph.D.s. They, however, will likely be weeded out of academic careers at the two-year, four-year, or six-year review stage of the tenure process, which gives highest weight to work that exhibits technical mastery, and little weight to policy issues related to judgment. Any economist who really tries to challenge the underlying foundations of the assumptions will almost assuredly be weeded out. Major contributions take gestation time and the tenure and promotion system in academic economic institutions does not allow such long gestation periods.

The result of this selectivity bias is that the interaction among the various types of students never materializes. Type BI candidates predominate in the profession, and the profession's approaches are not challenged by the contentious generalists or contentious mathematically-inclined students. This selection system causes the institutional structure to be self-reinforcing, and brings

about the current state of affairs in the profession. I am known as a critic of
graduate school; a major reason I am is that its screening weeds out individuals that I believe the profession needs.

CONCLUSION

The economics profession is not in a crisis. It is simply in a slow decline, as is
suggested by the declining number of US citizens receiving Ph.D.s in economics over the last twenty years. Eventually, the problems in the profession
will cause the current institutional structure to break down, or to change, to
better accommodate disagreement in judgment. But any change is unlikely to
occur anytime soon.

Nonetheless, the current institutional structure of the profession has short-
run costs. To be sincere in one's disagreements, as I believe economists are,
and simultaneously to hide the true nature of the disagreement requires a certain detachment from the analysis. Hiding the true nature of the disagreement
makes it impossible to arrive at intuitively satisfying resolutions to debates.
Moreover, it makes the resulting research less valuable than it could be.

Another effect of the institutional structure in the profession is that when it
strongly discourages disagreement based on judgment and sensibility, where
much of the disagreement about economic theory and policy resides, and encourages economists to surround themselves with like-minded economists,
rather than encouraging interaction and debate with economists who have
differing sensibilities and judgments, it leads to isolationism—geographical
pockets of agreement.

For example, in a survey asking students their views on the statement: "Can
fiscal policy be an effective tool in stabilizing policy?" only six percent of
Chicago students agreed with the statement; 60 percent of Yale students
strongly agreed with it. Or alternatively, 70 percent of the Chicago students
strongly agreed with the proposition that a minimum wage increases unemployment among young and unskilled workers; only 15 percent of Harvard
students strongly agreed to that. On a third issue, 84 percent of Chicago students strongly agreed with the proposition that inflation is primarily a monetary phenomenon; 7 percent of MIT students strongly agreed.[4] This cluster-
ing of agreements strongly suggests that the interchange of ideas is not taking
place, and that empirical work is not eliminating the disagreement.

It is my belief that a more open treatment of the reasons for disagreement
would encourage discussions to proceed beyond formal empirical testing, and
focus more on informal evidence. This more open treatment of reasons for
disagreement would accept that evidence will often be limited or inconclu-
sive, and that much disagreement is likely. But it would lead to more precise

statements of where and why economists disagree, and to more intuitively satisfying states of, if not resolutions of, debates.[5]

NOTES

1. A slam sheet is a list of reasons a professor should not use a competitor's book. Slam sheets are not compiled by most textbook authors; most prefer to highlight the strengths of their book. They are compiled by a few textbook authors whose egos and incomes are significantly intertwined with their own introductory books.
2. The competition among these competing paradigms need not be based on disagreement as much as on following different leads. By that I mean that a group considers the choices made by the other group to be legitimate, and complementary to their own approach.
3. The economic model of disagreement and the above discussion of the private costs and benefits of disagreeing cannot be applied to a "representative agent" model of economists. The reason is that there is a distribution of optimal disagreement in a field. The overall amount of disagreement depends on the character, independence of thought, personality, training, and ability of economists. An individual's optimal amount of disagreement depends on the total amount of agreement in the field. When most economists agree, there are enormous gains to be had in disagreeing. Thus, the odd contrarian can do very well for him or herself.
4. Arjo Klamer and David Colander, *The Making of an Economist*, 1990.
5. Part of the reason for this dismissing of fundamental critiques is the legitimate need to get on with what one is doing. In 1972, perhaps temporarily dismissing Basmann's critique made sense—in the hope that future work would show the attributes of the chosen path. But for decades, to have continued to ignore such criticisms, in spite of the failure of many econometric models, suggests a problem in the profession.

10. The Sounds of Silence: The Profession's Response to the COGEE Report

Oscar Wilde described a fox hunt as the unspeakable in pursuit of the inedible. Perhaps here (in graduate economics education) we have the overeducated in pursuit of the unknowable. —Robert Solow

When asked about the profession's response to the COGEE (Commission on Graduate Education in Economics) Report, Anne Krueger, the chair of the Commission, stated that if a pin dropped simultaneously with the issuance of the report, the dropping of the pin would sound like thunder. I agree; there has been essentially no response to the COGEE Report. Despite the lack of response, I nonetheless believe that there is something to say and be heard on the topic.

I'll begin with a discussion of the background of the COGEE report, why it came about, and what it had to say. Next, I consider the changes that have occurred in the profession over the last 10 years in relation to the COGEE Report. I conclude with some personal observations on the issues the COGEE Report raised.

THE BACKGROUND OF THE COGEE REPORT

The COGEE Report was a reaction to a general feeling of dissatisfaction at varying levels of the economics profession. Those concerns were prevalent all through the 1970s and early 1980s, and were articulated in Arjo Klamer's and my work on the profession. That joint work started in 1983 and led to a paper, "The Making of an Economist," in 1985 that was published in 1987 in the newly formed *Journal of Economic Perspectives*, a journal that was itself a product of that same discontent.[1]

In 1986, the ideas in our forthcoming paper were discussed at a National Science Foundation symposium, and it was felt that there was sufficient concern to create COGEE. Robert Eisner, then president of the AEA, set up the Commission with the charge to "take stock of what is being done (in graduate education), what results we are getting. . . . In all of this . . . the concern is, of course, very largely with the direction of research and focus of resources."

The Commission was to look more deeply at graduate education than Klamer and I had done. While there was a general agreement that what we had reported was, in general, correct, our work was certainly not systematic. (We had financed our limited surveys ourselves, with help from small grants from our schools.) COGEE was a much larger fact-finding effort, with substantial NSF funding. It was felt that a Commission made up of leading economists, basing their assessment on a more systematically structured study than ours, would provide more insight into what was really going on, and, if it was felt change was necessary, could better articulate those changes that were necessary. It was also felt that, if changes were necessary, the Commission would carry more weight in bringing about changes. Thus, COGEE was appointed with representatives of the top graduate schools and one government economist.[2] Lee Hansen oversaw the statistical work that underlaid the Commission's work.

In its makeup the Commission was broadly sympathetic to reform, although there was diversity of views represented, as necessarily had to be the case if the Commission were to be seen as representative of the mainstream graduate position. To reduce political infighting it was decided that the report would not be an official report of the AEA, but instead a report that reflected the views of the members and nothing more. Still, given the distinguished stature of the Commission members, it was felt that they and their report would make a difference.

Before the Commission's report, I had predicted, in print, that it would find that all was generally well with the profession, but that there were some areas for concern. I was partially right. Towards its beginning the report stated that "the current state of the profession is healthy." But I was pleasantly surprised by the depth in which the Commission considered the concerns of critics of the profession, and the relatively, for a Commission, strong recommendations it made.

The Commission's recommendations, which were issued in 1990 and published in September 1991 (Krueger *et al.* 1991), were the following:

1. Reasonable requirements in mathematics, statistics, and economics be established.
2. Remedial courses be offered to those who have deficiencies in economics, mathematics, or statistics.
3. Core courses be taught in a way that can balance breadth and depth, with sufficient attention to applications and real-world linkages to encourage students themselves to start applying the concepts.
4. The core be regarded as a departmental "public good" and its content be the concern of the entire department.

5. Field courses should attempt to include more empirical applications.
6. Greater attention should be given to writing and communication skills.
7. Efforts should be made to ease the transition from course work to dissertation.
8. More differentiation should exist among departments.

RESPONSE OF THE PROFESSION TO THE COGEE REPORT

I will discuss the profession's response to the COGEE report in two separate parts—changes at highly-ranked schools, and changes at lower-ranked schools.[3] By highly-ranked schools I mean the 20 or so schools who think of themselves in the top 10. (There are a variety of rankings; each school focuses on whichever ranking that ranks it highly, so more than ten schools see themselves in the top 10.) These top 10 are themselves divided into sub-groups that can vary somewhat; one does not, however, see large movements in rankings of schools. The existing rankings are reinforced by hiring practices. If a lower-ranked school seems to have hired an up-and-coming star, that star will receive offers from various top 10 schools. Usually, he or she will accept one of these offers, thereby preserving the initial ranking. (Graduate schools have no reserve clause in their contracts.)

For the most part the hiring practices of top 10 schools are incestuous; most hiring by top 10 schools is from other top 10 schools. If you are not sending your graduates to other top 10 schools, you will soon be out of the top 10. Not only do the top 10 schools supply professors to other top 10 schools; they also supply the majority of professors to programs that teach in graduate programs in economics. So, what goes on at these schools is central to graduate education in economics.

CHANGES AT HIGHLY RANKED-SCHOOLS

I will discuss changes at the highly-ranked schools in reference to each recommendation.

1. To my knowledge no school has changed its mathematical requirements in response to the Commission Report. No school that I know of has lowered its requirements. If anything, mathematical requirements have been raised. (The majority of the Commission members felt that at their school the level of mathematical sophistication needed by incoming graduate students had increased.)

Moreover, the underlying culture has continued to de-emphasize reading the literature and studying economic issues outside a formal theorem-proof and technical model approach. History of thought and history of economics requirements have declined further. Moreover, graduate school culture lets students know that they should de-emphasize these courses and focus on the "hard-core" core courses. For example, at one top 10 school that had a core economic history requirement, I was told that either the requirement was overlooked, or students were told to minimize their studying in the course to free up time for their other core courses.

2. Most schools already offered remedial courses in mathematics, so there was little change here. Most of these courses are given in August preceding the first semester. As Alan Blinder remarked, "We have always had 'remedial' math. (In fact it is pretty advanced.) We still do." From informal discussion, I would say that the content of these remedial courses has changed to a larger focus on game theory and dynamics. This change in focus has been in reaction to changes in the math used in the core economic courses.

No school, to my knowledge, had a remedial program in economics before the COGEE report, and none has implemented one. This is the case even though many new graduate students have taken few if any economics courses. (Some have taken none.) It is still possible to do exceptionally well in the first two years in economics graduate programs without having taken undergraduate economics. For those students without an undergraduate degree in economics this means that their economics training consists of the economics content of the core courses, and what they have learned on their own. When I asked one COGEE member about this I was told that most of the graduate students serve as teaching assistants in a principles course, and they learn economics there.

3. Most Commission members felt that the emphasis on technique and intuitive application has remained roughly the same or even increased. Some graduate students told me that they are encouraged to think of applying the models they learn. They are told to work on a paper in their first year, but they find doing that difficult because they have not had any in-class training in how to do so. Core classes generally consist of developing theorems, proofs of those theorems, studying techniques used in technical model building, and studying techniques used in formal testing of those models.

While the general focus on technique has remained constant, the techniques being learned are changing. Much more game theory is being taught, and being made central to the core of the micro courses. This movement toward game theory makes the core more closely applicable to real-world events, since it allows a broader range of assumptions. This change, however, has not been in reaction to the COGEE Report; it has been part of the continuing evolution of microeconomics thinking.

4. The teaching of the core has changed, not to a "public good" as recommended by the Commission, but instead to a "subdivided private good." By this I mean that instead of one individual teaching the core course, as was common in the past, core courses are now taught by combinations of two or three professors. Essentially, the core courses now consist of a collection of mini courses, each focusing on a separate area or modeling technique. These mini courses are separable; each professor sets the exam for his or her portion of the course. In one sense, this approach presents the students with more diversity, but in another, it removes any chance that a student might get an overall vision of the subject matter of the course. It increases the focus on the training in techniques. The development of these mini courses has, in many ways, eliminated the micro/macro distinction, and one school, Stanford, has integrated the two while simultaneously developing departmental guidelines as to what will be taught in the subsections of the core.

    To my knowledge, there are no integrative core courses, which provide an overview of the economics, given at any top school. History of thought requirements and electives have been eliminated at most top schools, and older professors who took an integrative approach to teaching are generally assigned non-core courses to teach. Where such courses still exist, students are discouraged from focusing on them.

5. I have no direct knowledge of whether significant changes in field courses have been made. My impression is that there has been a slight movement toward more applications, but that this change is primarily due to the changing of the core toward game theory.

6. Some Commission members said that at their schools, in workshops more emphasis is being given to writing. Some schools have developed a second-year field paper and students present their papers. Alan Blinder summed up the view of many when he wrote, "We keep experimenting with various types of workshops, papers, etc., but nothing works terribly well, and on the whole, it is much the same." So I would judge that attempts are being made to improve writing. These attempts, however, have been ongoing, and are not in response to the COGEE Report.

7. Here again I have little direct information, but based on general discussion with graduate professors, I feel that attempts are being made to improve the transition from course work to dissertation. One Commission member stated that at his school there is more assignment of advisors if the graduate student fails to develop ideas on his or her own. At some schools workshops and luncheon seminars are required in the third year;

these are meant to focus the attention of the student on developing a thesis topic. Recently the Social Science Research Council has started a program, including summer workshops and fellowships, to encourage more focus on intuitive foundations.

8.   Among top schools there has been no recognizable movement toward differentiation. If anything, the process has gone the other way. When Klamer and I did our initial study, there was a significant difference in top schools, reflected in differences in what students believed. These differences reflected the view of some major professor there who taught the core. With recent hires blending freshwater and saltwater schools, and the division of the core courses into components, such differences in beliefs among schools are far less noticeable. This is (1) because there are fewer differences in the profession, and (2) because even if there are differences, those differences will not be taught to the students because the core courses are divided among two or three professors focusing on the particular sub-area of that course within which they work.

CHANGES AT OTHER SCHOOLS

Graduate economics education involves much more than these élite schools. In fact, there are some 150 graduate programs in economics. I estimate that as more schools assign "top 10" status to themselves, there are an additional 30 or so schools in the top 25, so essentially there are 50 schools in the top 25. Although I have not formally studied the issue, from informal discussion I would say that the reactions to the COGEE Report discussed above generally carry over to these additional 30 schools. Their tenure criteria are generally modifications of those at higher-level schools, and most of the hiring of professors for these 50 top 25 schools is done from the top 10 schools. They hire the "second tier" of the top 10 schools' students who are looking for graduate teaching jobs. Their students, along with other top 10 school students who chose a non-academic option, or who did not get offers for academic jobs in graduate programs, will find jobs at the Fed, government, business, international organizations, or liberal arts colleges, or will return to their home country.[4] Thus, the 50 schools in the top 25 make a relatively closed set.[5] They hire from each other; they tend to cover the same issues, and they approach economics in the same way. The hiring process pushes strongly toward uniformity of approach.

The 100 or so programs that do not bother with top 10 ranking have various raisons d'être. Some are regional schools, which provide professors and policy economists for particular areas. Some are *special approach* schools, and others are simply programs that exist primarily on paper as a supplement to a

Masters Program. These schools often teach economics in a somewhat different way than do the top 25 schools. Some of these programs are distinctively different; some are clones of the higher-level schools; and others are eclectic. Almost none of their graduates are hired at top 25 schools, but many go on to teach at undergraduate schools, and work in various aspects of business and government and non-government agencies. As was the case with top 25 schools, foreign students make up a majority of the student body.

Klamer's and my original study focused only on the top 10 programs; COGEE focused heavily on the first two of my groups—the 50 schools in the top 25.[6] Thus, this third group, about 100 schools, has gone almost completely unstudied. I have, however, informally discussed the problems with professors at a number of these schools, and have found them much more open to discussion of change than the faculties at top 25 schools. This is both because they are less satisfied with their programs, and because they often have a hard time placing their students in acceptable jobs. Thus, at this level there are ongoing demand-driven changes.

Some of these schools have narrowed their offerings and focused on individual areas where they have a comparative strength. For example, Rensselaer Polytechnic Institute (RPI) has an interesting program that focuses entirely on environmental and evolutionary economics, building on its strength as an engineering school. Doing this, they have been able to recruit a high quality student body. The University of New Hampshire has focused on preparing students to teach at liberal arts programs, and has an innovative teaching cognate, which graduate students can choose. It requires a history of thought course and has broad-based overview courses that help provide the broad-based vision professors at liberal arts colleges need.

The University of Kentucky and the University of Cincinnati have established seminars on teaching for graduate students, taught by professors whose tenure decision will be based on teaching as well as on research. The University of Hawaii focuses on Pacific Rim issues. George Mason, Auburn, Notre Dame, the New School, U.C. Riverside, and Utah maintain programs with a special emphasis on a particular approach to economics. Among these schools, diversity exists. These schools, however, have little influence on the top 25 and on what happens in the profession. I know of no recent case where one of their graduates was hired by a top 25 school; thus their ideas do not become integrated into the standard approach.

Two aspects of this diversity should be noted. The first is that the diversity has not increased, and, indeed, may have decreased, since there has been an increased focus on teaching mathematical techniques at many "non-mainstream" programs so as to intensify the perceived rigor of their programs. Second, many of the changes that have occurred since the COGEE Report have been in response to university-wide pressures, rather than to pressures from within an economics department. For example, the programs focusing on teaching at the University of Kentucky and at the University of New Hampshire were started by the university, and economics departments then chose to participate.

MY PERSONAL VIEW OF THE CHANGES

The above discussion makes it quite clear that the changes that have occurred in graduate education in response to the COGEE Report have been minimal. Despite this lack of response, I detect less concern about the state of graduate economics education than there was in the 1970s and 1980s. The reason for this is twofold.

One reason is that the core of formal economics is changing away from static perfectly competitive analysis and toward dynamic non-perfectly competitive analysis. Advances in areas such as nonlinear dynamics, evolutionary game theory, and time series econometrics have broadened the intuitive applicability of the core that students are learning. These advances allow a broader set of assumptions to be made, and thus allow the development of more potentially relevant formal models. In the development of formal theory, I detect a new excitement of discovery.

As discussed by Solow (1997) most economists are not involved in developing formal theory; they are involved in technical model building, and in relating the models they develop to data. Solow correctly points out that there is a major difference between the two. The first is pure theory; the second is applied model building.

In discussing this applied technical theory Solow argues that there is a tendency for these technical models to exceed the data available to test them. He writes:

> In economics, model-builders' busywork is to refine their ideas to ask questions to which the available data cannot give the answer. Econometric theorists invent methods to estimate parameters about which the data have no information. . . . As the models become more refined, the signal-to-noise ratio in the data becomes very attenuated. Since no empirical verdict is forthcoming, the student goes back to the drawing board—and refines the idea even more. (p. 57)

He concludes this discussion with the nutshell quoted at the beginning of this chapter, significantly questioning the usefulness of much of the applied work that is done in economics. But he ends his critical discussion of the state of economics by summing up: "But it sure beats the alternatives."[7]

A second reason there is less concern about the state of graduate economics education is that this advance in formal theory has been accompanied by a change in the student body—in who is becoming, and has become, an economist. As better information about what graduate education in economics is has spread through the profession, the selection process is distilling a higher proportion of students who are comfortable with a formal and highly technical approach. Individuals who do not feel at ease with this technical approach are choosing not to apply, and the selection process is eliminating some others who do apply.[8] This selection process has already made a significant change in the structure of the profession from what it was twenty years ago.

The below-age-45 professors are now almost all highly technical economists who are comfortable with the existing situation. Given current selection procedures, in 20 years almost all criticism of the profession will come from without rather than within since potential critics will never enter the profession.[9]

In the eyes of most graduate school professors, this selection process is increasing the quality of admitted students. For these professors, abilities and mindsets are unidimensional, and measurable by students' ability to excel in doing formal proofs of abstract theorems. Those who don't excel in doing formal proofs go on to do technical applied work, and the applied work we get from them is technically superior to previous applied work.

My view is different; I regard abilities and mindsets as multidimensional. Moreover, I believe that often there is a low correlation between the mindset needed to do good applied work in economics—pushing the frontiers of the application of economic theory—and the mindset needed to push out the frontiers of formal economic theory.

Pushing the frontiers of formal economic theory requires what might be called a formalist deductivist mindset. It is a highly disciplined mindset that is most comfortable with theorem/proof understanding of issues. Formalists can often be creative, but it is a creativity in a perfectionist mold; it wants every piece in order. Formalists usually have the ability to remove themselves from the real world; they can structure abstract proofs in abstract settings. It is a mindset that is useful in a number of settings, including abstract mathematics and formal logic. Being a good formalist requires a combination of abstract creativity and a precise mind. Gerard Debreu is an example of a brilliant economic formalist.

Doing creative applied work requires a quite different mindset—what I call a generalist inductivist mindset. It is a mindset that is superb at observing the world around it, and incorporating those observations in its understanding of the world. A generalist can see patterns in a real-world setting, and can choose what is important and what is not. This mindset often leads the person to see the forest, while leaving the trees out of focus. Once a generalist's intuition sees an answer, he or she often has no patience for formally dotting i's or crossing t's. Creative applied work requires these generalist inductivist skills.

A good generalist can push the informal frontiers of economics, but he or she cannot push out the formal frontiers. Examples of economic generalists are Douglass North and James Buchanan.

Technical applied work is the most difficult branch of economics. To do it well one must be both a good generalist and a good formalist. Good technical applied work requires the common sense intuition of a generalist and the highly disciplined perfectionism of a formalist. Few economists embody this combination. Ken Arrow, Amaryta Sen, and Robert Solow come to mind as economists who do rank highly in both dimensions.

Most individuals rank much higher in one mindset than the other. Individuals who have one mindset can still work in the other, but they find it difficult to do creative work outside their own mindset. It is like writing poetry in a language that is not one's own. One can do it, but the output is unlikely to be creative. It is for that reason that short, remedial courses in mathematics do nothing to solve the problem. In fact, they make it worse because they set the tone for the core courses, and convey a ranking of students that puts generalist knowledge down.[10]

SOLOW'S MISTAKE

It is because of this two-dimensional set of abilities that I see a problem with graduate economics education. Put simply, the selection process is eliminating individuals with generalist inductivist proclivities from the profession. In doing so, it has created precisely the problem Solow says exists in the profession. He seems to assume implicitly that all economists are as balanced in both dimensions as he is. They are not, and as the profession gravitates more and more toward formalist deductivists, the common-sense anchor on applied work has been removed because of the current nature of graduate economics education.

Let me be clear about how I see this process working. All students entering the top graduate schools in economics are extremely bright—sufficiently bright so that the formalist/generalist distinction I am making does not show up on GRE math scores. Similarly, at the level of intelligence I am talking about, the generalist students entering graduate school can meet the requirements set in the core courses. They can do so because, while the qualifying core exams generally look impressive, they do not test the creative element of working in the formalist mode. That creative element would involve an exam that demanded structuring an approach to a new problem, not replicating a proof that was presented in class, or repeating a variation of an exercise that was presented in class, which is what the core exams that I have seen do. This suspicion is strengthened by the fact that in all cases that I explored, *the core exam is made up by the same individual who gave that portion of the course.* Core exams are essentially just another course exam; they do not test a deep understanding of the material.[11]

Thus, at least from the feedback I have gotten, it is not the fact that the core is too hard or too mathematical that is keeping generalists out of graduate school; it is the fact that the core is imposing a cost that generalists are unwilling to bear. Their alternatives are too good since businesses and government agencies find bright generalists highly attractive.

A PROPOSAL

I am a realist; I do not expect graduate economics programs to change. Thus I see applied economists gravitating more and more to public policy schools and interdisciplinary programs. As the rigor and selectivity of these schools and programs increase, more and more of the demand for applied economists will come from them, not from graduate economics programs. Graduate economics Ph.D. programs will not only fail to grow as they have failed to do in the past 20 years; they will shrink.

Despite the slight chance of the situation actually changing, let me nonetheless offer a proposal that I think could improve applied work in economics at little cost to the development of formal theory. The proposal is for one or more of the top schools to modify its graduate program so that that program is more attractive to generalist students. They could do this by changing the core exams in the following way:

> Instead of being prepared by the individuals teaching the course, the core exams would be prepared and graded by a group of individuals who work in the area where the student believes he or she would like to work.

For example, there might be two tracks, one for those planning to extend formal theory and another for those planning to find jobs in undergraduate teaching, business, or government. The core exam testing students' ability to extend formal theory would be set by a group of top graduate economics professors (not those teaching the course). The core exam for others would be set by a combination of top business and government personnel and undergraduate professors. There are many variations of this proposal, but the key elements of it are that (1) the core exam is determined by a person or persons other than the professors who teach the course, and (2) there are at least two different tracks that graduate students could follow.

The proposal would not be especially difficult to implement. (The British system has, until recently, been built around outside examiners, and field exams and dissertation defenses have often included outside examiners.) It would even be possible that the same core courses, taught in the same way as now, could be offered. However, an additional part would need to be added to each of the core courses—a part that would provide the training a generalist needs, which is an overview of the field. This additional part would likely cover the debates that are currently going on, the recent history of those debates, and where the research that is currently being done fits in those debates. Unlike other sections of the core that are taught in mini courses, this part could be spread over the entire semester, and have significant amounts of reading. That reading could possibly be specified by the group of professors who would serve as examiners for that part of the core exams.

This overview part of the core courses would become a central part of the generalist track's education, and play a significant role in the generalist track core exam. The formalist track would be like the material covered in current core exams, but much more demanding, because even higher standards could be required since generalists would not have to be provided with a crutch to get through the course. Students could choose to do one, or both, of these core qualifying exams, depending on what their desired employment is.

As I envision it, the formalist core exam would require the creative development and use of formalist tools while the generalist core exam would be much more like the qualifying exams of 20 or 30 years ago. It would involve an understanding of the formal developments, but would not require students to replicate formal theorems and proofs, or replicate technical models. Instead, it would require students to interpret and understand the literature in the field, the limitations of the theory, and the evolution of thinking in that field, and to do technical work at the level that business economists, government economists, or most professors actually do.

Creating such a different track will not have a significant cost to formal research. Most of the professors at top 20 schools that I have talked to agreed that, in reality, only about one-fourth of their students were of the caliber to have any chance of making a real contribution to formal theory. The other students are there primarily to fill up the classes.

This plan will not change the profession quickly. The selection process that determines the nature of the profession works much more slowly. But it will help address the current imbalance in the profession, and perhaps, over time, lead to a healthier and stronger profession, one that Solow and the rest of us could characterize as "the appropriately educated pushing the boundaries of what is knowable."

NOTES

1. We later expanded the paper into a book (1990) with the same title.
2. The members of the Commission were: Anne Krueger, Kenneth Arrow, Olivier Blanchard, Alan Blinder, Claudia Goldin, Edward Leamer, Robert Lucas, Jan Panzar, Rudolph Penner, Paul Schultz, Joseph Stiglitz, and Lawrence Summers.
3. This discussion is based on a survey of COGEE Commission members and informal discussions with friends in the profession. It is not based on hard evidence, but it is, I believe, correct in its essentials.
4. At these graduate schools, students are told that teaching at a graduate school is what it is all about. Other job alternatives are portrayed as less exciting, and less prestigious. A few students who find themselves in graduate schools favoring non-graduate academic appointments nevertheless remain steadfast, but the majority succumb to the pressure. It should also be noted that more than 50 percent of the students in graduate economics programs are foreign students. This is both because foreign students tend to be better prepared technically and are thus selected over American students, and because top US students are choosing other alternatives.
5. There are exceptions. For example, Washington University still maintains an institutional focus, and U. Mass-Amherst maintains a radical focus.
6. Lee Hansen reported that the sampling methodology used was heavily weighted toward the top schools. All top schools were included; about one fifth of the bottom half of the top 91 schools were included. No school ranked lower than 91 was included.
7. I believe Solow's nutshell captures criticism such as my view of the situation in the economics profession in the 1990s and early 2000s. Where we differ is in our judgment of whether the situation beats the unspecified alternatives.
8. I have discussed this issue in more detail in Colander (1996).
9. Looking at incoming graduate Ph.D. classes, one sees that many incoming students in top 25 schools are math rather than economics majors and an increasing number have the equivalent of M.A.s or more in mathematics when entering.
10. Edward Leamer compared the current situation in graduate economics education to a school for the deaf (mathematically) that insists on oral language (mathematics) even though few students or even teachers can speak it.
11. As one top mathematical economist who has taught at a true top 10 school told me, he can walk around campus and have students come up to him and recite fixed-point theorems. He feels that 20 percent really understand what is going on in the theorem, but he feels that none of them have a clue about the implications of the idea for economics.

PART VI

The Future of the Economics Profession

11. The Death of NeoClassical Economics*

The term, neoClassical economics, was born in 1900; in this chapter I am proposing economist-assisted terminasia. By the powers vested in me as president of the History of Economics Society, I hereby declare the term, neoClassical economics, dead.[1] Let me be clear about what I am sentencing to death—it is not the content of neoClassical economics. As I will discuss below, it is difficult to determine what that content is, and even if I wanted to kill the content, I have no role in determining content. The role of historians of thought is to record, not determine, content. What I am declaring dead is the term.

Historians of thought, especially those of us who write textbooks and teach, have some influence over terminology. One of our important jobs is to provide students and non-specialists with insight into what the content of economics is. One of the ways we do so is through classifying—creating terminology that provides students and non-specialists an entree into debates that would otherwise be too complicated to understand. We adopt classifying terminology and give it definitional content. It is historians of thought who are the primary arbiters of descriptive terminology and hence we can have a role in changing that terminology. Therein lies the basis for my lethal decree.

ON CLASSIFICATION

Classifying is not for the faint of heart nor the perfectionist; it requires you to mix what, in a deeper sense, are unmixables, to blend into composites that which does not blend. When you do this, you've got to hold your nose to avoid the resulting reaction, both from researchers who feel mistreated and from other historians of thought who rightly point out the innumerable sensibilities the classification has violated. But classification is necessary, and what we hope is that, with the classification, those students who don't go on to further studies will have a better understanding than they otherwise would have had, and that those students who continue their studies will learn the problems with the classifications, transcend them, and forgive us our compromises that mislead.

151

Historians of thought have seldom given serious specific consideration to the general characteristics of good classification.[2] Should one focus on temporal dimensions? Should one use terms that tie together the similarities, or terms that emphasize the differences? What is the ideal terminology?

While I certainly don't have the answers to these questions, I do have a few observations and suggestions. The first observation is that since classifications are usually employed to compare one set of thoughts with another, there is one degree of freedom in making classifications. This means that the reference school can be called anything. For example, the longevity of the term, Classical, is not so much because the term is good, but is more because it has been the numeraire for other classifications. The neoClassical and New Classical classifications only make sense in relation to Classical, but in itself "Classical" could have been anything. Had economics chosen a different reference term we could be talking about "the New Ricardians" or the "neoMarketeers."

The second observation is that most of the classifications economists use have developed serendipitously. A term is used and repeated by a couple of people, and suddenly it is "in use." Such serendipitous terminology generally has a short-run focus—it refers to what immediately preceded it. That's why we see lots of new, neo, new neo, and post (with and without hyphens) modifications of school names.

Let me suggest five classification criteria that I think are important:

1. *A classification should help organize thinking about the issues to which it refers and it should do so in a way that is understandable to the non-specialist.*
    The reasoning for this criterion is fairly obvious. The whole purpose of the classification is to help non-specialists understand complicated debates. Based on this criterion, the term "Classical" is not an especially good term.
2. *A classification should seem natural and intuitive to most practitioners, and acceptable to those thus classified.*
    Ultimately, assuming we are talking about an existing school, it is the individuals being classified who will have to say whether a classification captures their thinking. If they object to it, it will not be likely to last. Luckily, when historians are classifying historical schools, most practitioners are dead, and cannot object.
3. *A classification should work well over time.*
    Classifications that are most useful remain appropriate over a fairly long period of time. This criterion does not bode well for any classification with the prefix new or neo. Seen against a short-term horizon, defining something as "new whatever" makes a lot of sense, since people have a good idea of what "whatever" is. But as time goes by, that "whatever" is

forgotten and the "new whatever" is less clear. Moreover, what is new in one time period soon becomes old. But, when that happens, the classification often has become sufficiently accepted that it is part of the language, and difficult to replace. To describe the next development you've got to move to "new new," "neonew," or maybe "neoneo." The same problems exist with the terms modern and post-modern.

4. *A classification should be used to describe content, not to harbor some ideological agenda.*
   The argument for this proposition is, again, fairly obvious; one wants a general criterion that is as value-neutral as possible. The "Dummies" would not be a good classification.

5. *A classification should have a consistent definition.*
   Classifications exhibit network-externality characteristics. The value of the term is in the image, the set of articles and ideas, that a term brings up in people's minds. A good classification has a standard definition, so when people hear it, they know what is meant by it. It should not mean different things to different people. When a single classification means different things to different people, confusion will result.

If a classification doesn't meet these five criteria it will clutter the terminological landscape; if it does, then the name can serve a useful purpose: It can complete a picture, and make clear not only the ideas of the group being described, but, like the final piece of a puzzle, also make the others' body of work clearer. Otherwise, the classification will confuse, not clarify. Just as a piece of a puzzle in the wrong place will obscure a picture rather than complete it, so, too, will a loosely-used term.

All fields have classification problems. In art, for example, one finds some good classifications: impressionism, expressionism, and minimalist bring to mind the art to which the terms are referring. Of course, art has some bad classifications too. Who knows what is meant by modern or post-modern?[3]

WHY THE NEOCLASSICAL CLASSIFICATION SHOULD DIE

Given my acknowledgment of the problems of any classification system, the problems with the term neoClassical must be especially onerous to deserve its death. In my view they are. The use of the term, neoClassical, to describe the economics that is practiced today is not only not useful, but it actually hinders understanding by students and lay people of what contemporary economics is. The term may still have a role in intertemporal comparisons, but, if it is to do so, it is even more important to have the neoClassical era end at some point.[4] Economics has changed enormously from 1870 to now, and is continually changing. To serve an intertemporal purpose, the term, "neoClassical economics school," has to die.

Let me be clear about what I see as the largest problem with the use of the term. That is its use by some heterodox economists, by many non-specialists, and by historians of thought at unguarded moments, as a classifier for the approach that the majority of economists take today. We all, me included, fall into the habit of calling modern economics "neoClassical" when we want to contrast modern mainstream economics with heterodox economics. When we like the alternative, the neoClassical term is often used as a slur, with our readers, or listeners, knowing what we mean. Of course, historians of thought are far better at avoiding this "slur" use than are others. The worst use, and the place one hears the term "neoClassical" most often, is in the discussions by lay people who object to some portion of modern economic thought. To them bad economics and neoClassical economics are synonymous terms.

There is much not to like in current economics; but slurring it by calling it neoClassical economics does not add to students' understanding of the current failings of economics. Economists today are not neoClassical according to any reasonable definition of the term. They are far more eclectic, and concerned with different issues, than were the economists of the early 1900s that the term was originally designed to describe. If we don't like modern economics, we should say so, but we should not take the easy road, implicitly condemning modern economics by the terminology we choose.

EVOLUTION OF THE TERM, NEOCLASSICAL

The story of the evolution of the term, neoClassical, is a story of metamorphosis. Let me briefly recount its history. The root term, Classical, was coined by Marx (1847) as a description of Ricardo's formal economics. Marx contrasted Classical with vulgar, or romantic, economics, by both of which terms he meant "economics close to the people." Various writers used the "Classical" terminology and, as they did, the term eventually became a general classifier for the economics of the period running somewhere between 1776 and 1870. Thus we could talk about the evolution of thinking from the mercantilist to the Classical period.

Historians of thought have raised numerous issues about the use of the term, Classical. One issue is : When did the Classical period begin? Schumpeter (1954), following Marx, starts the Classical era with Ricardo. He places Adam Smith with the mercantilist pamphleteers, taking the Classical period as 1790 to 1879.[5] Most histories of thought include Smith as a Classical economist. Most writers put the end of the Classical period a bit earlier—in 1870—and start the neoClassical period with Menger, but such beginning and ending issues, unless they involve a writer of the stature of Smith, are of minor importance. Another issue is whether a single term can encompass such disparate thinkers as Smith and Ricardo. In some ways it would have been much more helpful to have had a separate Smithian school whose focus was on growth, and a separate Ricardian school whose focus was on distributive shares.

FROM CLASSICAL TO NEOCLASSICAL

In the 1870s there was a qualitative change in some economists' approach to doing economics. During this time utilitarianism and marginalism rose in importance, and deductive models with utilitarian foundations became more fashionable. To capture this change, it was helpful to develop a new classification to distinguish that approach from the earlier Classical approaches based on the labor, or cost, theories of value. The term that developed was neoClassical.

The term, neoClassical, was initially coined by Thorstein Veblen (1900) in his "Preconceptions of Economic Science."[6] As Veblen used the term, it was a negative description of Marshall's economics, which itself was a type of synthesis of the marginalism found in Menger and Jevons with broader Classical themes in Smith, Ricardo, and Mill. Thus, from the beginning, the term was used by an outsider to characterize the thinking of another group. When Veblen coined it, it was not meant as a description of mainstream economics. In the early 1900s, economics was divided, and, in the United States at least, neoClassical thought was not mainstream; institutionalism was more embedded than neoClassical thought. Veblen's terminology caught on and the term, neoClassical, came into general use and can be found in the writings of Mitchell (1967), Hobson (1925), and Roll (1938, 1942).

Hicks (1932, 1934) and Stigler (1941) extended the meaning of neoClassical to encompass all marginalist writers, including Menger, Jevons, and J.B. Clark. Most writers after Hicks and Stigler used the term inclusively. Thus it lost most of its initial meaning. Instead of describing Marshallian economics, it became associated with the use of calculus, the use of marginal productivity theory, and a focus on relative prices. As has been noted by a number of authors, while the neoClassical terminology makes some sense for Marshall, who emphasized the connection of his approach with the Classical approach, it makes far less sense for the others, such as Jevons, who emphasized the difference between his views and those of the Classicals. Some have suggested that anti-Classical would have been preferable.

Keynes (1936), as was his way, disregarded existing usage, and developed his own. He lumped Classicals and neoClassicals together, calling them all

Classicals, suggesting that the distinctions in pre-Keynesian work were of minor importance. Keynes' use added yet another dimension to the Classical classification; it was a term that was to be contrasted with Keynesian. In the third edition of his principles textbook Samuelson (1955) built on Keynes' classification and turned it around on Keynes by developing the neoClassical synthesis. In the neoClassical synthesis, Keynes' dispute with Classical economists was resolved. This use of the term "neoClassical" as an alternative to Keynesian models provides another confusion because it adds another reference point that brings to mind different elements of thought than would other comparisons.

CURRENT USE OF THE TERM

The most lavish users of the term "neoClassical" are heterodox economists. (I can always tell when I am around heterodox economists by the number of times I hear the term, neoClassical.) For the most part, mainstream economists don't use the term; when they do, it is used almost unthinkingly, as in "neoClassical growth theory" or in "neoClassical synthesis."

The current use of the term by historians of thought is schizophrenic and inconsistent. Most books follow Stigler's lead and include Jevons, Marshall, Walras, Menger, and similar writers as neoClassical economists, thus starting the neoClassical period in 1870 and ending it around 1930. Consistent with this usage, many history of economic thought texts, mine included, are divided into sections: Pre-Classical, Classical, neoClassical, and Modern.

That use has its problems, but they fall within the normal set of problems of any classification. My objections to the term, neoClassical, involve its use to juxtapose modern mainstream economics with heterodox economics, which is another use historians of economic thought make of the neoClassical classification.

Let me give a couple of examples. Backhouse (1985) discusses the neoClassical period as extending from 1890 to 1939. (It is one of his central divisions.) He contrasts that period with the modern period. But then he concludes his book by contrasting modern economics with heterodox economics. There, he talks about "a neoClassical research program" and writes, "for all its limitations, and there are many, neoClassical economics has, over the past century, been successfully applied to an ever-wider range of problems" (1985, p. 414). Somehow, neoClassical economics didn't end in 1939, but became merged with modern economics.

In their text Ekelund and Hebert (1997) emphasize the early work of Cournot and Dupuit in their discussion of neoClassical economics. Thus their neoClassical period starts at about 1840. They are unclear as to where it ends;

they trace the development of "early neoClassical economics," a term that suggests that there is a "later period." They continue that view in the discussion of 20th century paradigms where they state that "neoClassical economics blossomed" (p. 404). Thus it would seem that neoClassical economics became the modern orthodoxy.

Brue (1994) distinguishes the marginalist school of Jevons and Menger from the neoClassical school of Marshall, Edgeworth, and Clark. NeoClassical economists include Chamberlin and Robinson. He then starts the "mathematical period" in 1935, although he states that "mathematical economics" does not constitute a separate school of economics (p. 361).

Blaug (1985) does not use the neoClassical term to describe marginalism, but he does use it in two ways, first when discussing macro theory (p. 632), and second when he is criticizing modern theory.[7]

As a textbook author, I am sympathetic to the inconsistent use of neoClassical. In popular parlance the term neoClassical is used in two quite separate ways: (1) to describe the economics from 1870 to the 1930s, and (2) to describe modern economics in reference to heterodox thinking today. Textbook authors have a natural tendency to use it in that same way. Unfortunately, the two uses make logical sense only if modern economics is essentially the same in the earlier time period as it is today. You can't have it both ways. Either modern economics is part of neoClassical economics or it isn't.

I quite agree that certain aspects of neoClassical economics remain as part of modern economics. That is true of any field—the new approach accepts certain parts of the previous approach. But, in my view, modern economics is fundamentally different from neoClassical economics, and, if students are to understand modern economics, they must understand that. In our choice of terminology it is more helpful to students to emphasize the differences between modern economics and neoClassical than it is to recognize the similarities.

Modern economics involves a broader world view and is far more eclectic than the neoClassical terminology allows. To capture that eclecticism, modern economics must be given a much broader, and more sympathetic, classification, including the penumbra surrounding the core ideas. Thus, the argument I am making is that, for outside observers to understand what is happening in economic thinking today, it is necessary to distinguish a new school of economics that can be contrasted with neoClassical economics in the same way that neoClassical economics was contrasted with Classical economics.

I am pronouncing the death of the terms but I'm not sure of the date we should give to the death of neoClassical economics itself. The most logical cutoff would be somewhere between 1935 and 2000. The date cannot be pinpointed because the death was gradual—a slow transition rather than a sudden epiphany. Game theory made its appearance in 1946. In many ways the two books that tied up the loose ends and captured the essence of neoClassical economics, Hicks' *Value and Capital* (1939), and Samuelson's *Foundations* (1947), were culminating works—they put all the pieces of marginalism together. Important work thereafter was modern. The very fact that the economics of the 1950s was able to include Keynesian economics as its macroeconomics demonstrates an enormous change in method, approach, and content of economics. Keynesian macroeconomics has few of the characteristics attributed to neoClassical economics.

I should make it clear that I am not alone in declaring the neoClassical terminology dead, and some historians of thought, such as Niehans, don't use the term at all. Even some of those who use it question its usefulness. For example, Mark Blaug writes: "NeoClassical economics transformed itself so radically in the 1940s and 1950s that someone ought to invent an entirely new label for post-war orthodox economics" (1998, p. 2).

Hicks, who helped broaden the use of the term to include all marginalists in his *Value and Capital,* had second thoughts, and in 1983 (pp. xiii–xiv) he suggested that the term, neoClassical, be killed. And finally, the two writers who have explored the history of the term in depth, Tony Aspromourgos (1986) and Susan Fayazmanesh (1998), both conclude that the term should die.

ATTRIBUTES OF THE NEOCLASSICAL SCHOOL

To make the comparison between neoClassical and modern more concrete, let me list briefly the primary attributes of neoClassical economics that are found in most history of thought texts, and contrast them with the primary attributes of modern economics.

1. *NeoClassical economics focuses on allocation of resources at a given moment in time.*
    This attribute is embodied in Robbins' definition —the allocation of scarce resources among alternative ends—which became the standard definition of neoClassical economics.
2. *NeoClassical economics accepts some variation of utilitarianism as playing a central role in understanding the economy.*
    The movement to demand and subjective choice theory, and away from supply considerations, was a hallmark of early neoClassical thought. While initially the focus was almost entirely on utilitarianism and demand, the focus quickly evolved to a view that demand was only one blade of the scissors.
3. *NeoClassical economics focuses on marginal tradeoffs.*
    NeoClassical economics came into existence as calculus spread to eco-

nomics, and its initial work was centered around the marginal tradeoffs that calculus focused on.

4. *NeoClassical economics assumes far-sighted rationality.*
    In order to structure the economic problem within a constrained maximization framework, one has to specify rationality in a way consistent with constrained optimization. Specific rationality assumptions quickly became central to the neoClassical approach.

5. *NeoClassical economics accepts methodological individualism.*
    This attribute, like the two before it, is closely tied to the constrained maximization approach. Someone must be doing the maximizing, and in neoClassical economics it was the individual. One starts with individual rationality, and the market translates that individual rationality into social rationality.

6. *NeoClassical economics is structured around a general equilibrium conception of the economy.*
    This last attribute is more debatable than the others. Schumpeter made the general equilibrium conception of the economy central to his definition of neoClassical economics. I agree it is important, but if it were absolutely central it would eliminate Marshall from the neoClassical school. However, Schumpeter is right in the following way: In order to make neoClassical economics more than an applied policy approach to problems (something Schumpeter wanted to do) one needs a general unique equilibrium conception of the economy. Formal welfare economics is based on this general equilibrium conception.

MODERN ECONOMICS AND THE SIX ATTRIBUTES

My argument against the use of the neoClassical term to describe modern economics is that modern economics does not require adherence to these six attributes. It is much more eclectic. The movement away from neoClassical economics can be traced to the 1930s when large components of neoClassical theory were being abandoned by cutting-edge theorists, as they attempted to forge a new economics.

Let me consider each of the six attributes, giving examples of where modern economics parts company with neoClassical economics.

1. *Focus on allocation of resources at a given moment in time.*
    The interest in allocation of resources at a given moment in time ended long ago; the problems solved. Been there, done that. The focus of research quickly turned to allocation over time. In the 1990s and early 2000s, for example, growth has been a key topic. New growth theory is

decidedly mainstream and decidedly non-neoClassical. In fact, it is generally contrasted with neoClassical growth theory.

2.   *Acceptance of utilitarianism.*
     Few modern economists today accept utilitarianism; most see it as a quaint aspect of the past. One sees very little operational use of utility theory in modern economics. Critics of my view might claim that, in principles and intermediate books, versions of utilitarianism still reign, but they are presented for pedagogical reasons, not because utilitarianism is the reigning approach of modern economists.

3.   *Focus on marginal tradeoffs.*
     While many undergraduate texts still present economics within a marginal framework, that is not the way it is presented in graduate schools or the way top economists think about issues. In fact, by the 1930s, in cutting-edge theory, calculus was already being dropped, having been mined for its insights, and math was moving to set theory and topology as economists tried to expand the domain of the economics to include a wider variety of topics. In modern graduate microeconomics, game theory has almost completely replaced calculus as the central modeling apparatus.

4.   *Assumption of far-sighted rationality.*
     The decrease in the focus on utilitarianism has been accompanied by a decrease in the far-sighted rationality assumption. In modern economics, bounded rationality, norm-based rationality (perhaps established through evolutionary game theory), and empirically-determined rationality are fully acceptable approaches to problems.

5.   *Methodological individualism.*
     While individualism still reigns, it is under attack by branches of modern economics. Complexity theorists challenge the entire individualistic approach, at least when that approach is used to understand the aggregate economy. Evolutionary game theorists are attempting to show how such norms develop and constrain behavior. New Institutionalists consistently operate out of a framework at odds with methodological individualism.

6.   *General equilibrium.*
     The existence of a unique general equilibrium is still the predominantly–held view, but that is primarily because general equilibrium models are seldom used. In theory, multiple equilibria work is ongoing, and equilibrium selection mechanisms are an important element of study. Schumpeter made the existence of a single equilibrium the requirement of science and neoClassical economics never seriously considered the problem of multiple equilibria.[8] In modern economics, theoretical economists are quite willing to consider multiple equilibria, as can be seen in the work

of Woodward (1991) and many others. It is true that modern work in policy generally avoids any discussion of multiple equilibria, and that is one of the contradictions in modern economics, but the multiple equilibria topic is no longer out of bounds.

TOP MODERN ECONOMISTS

My argument is not that neoClassical economic ideas are not still used; they are. My argument is only that they are not constraining attributes; they are not requirements of what a current economist must do to have a reasonably good chance for success. One can work in a quite different vein and still be considered mainstream. Consider the following names: David Romer, William Brock, Richard Thaler, William Baumol, George Akerlof, Joe Stiglitz, David Card, Alan Krueger, Paul Krugman, Ken Arrow, Amartya Sen, Thomas Shelling. . . I could go on, but these should make my point. Each is considered a top modern economist, but each operates outside the "neoClassical framework" in portions of his work.

Now one could argue that the economists listed above are actually heterodox economists who are deviating from the neoClassical core that is modern economics. But such an argument would be wrong. First, these researchers do not see themselves as heterodox economists, and thus classifying them as heterodox would violate the criterion that a classification should be acceptable to its practitioners. Second, all of them are highly respected economists with jobs at, or offers from, top graduate schools. If "heterodox" is to be meaningful, it should be defined as an approach to problems that is not accepted as legitimate. Thus, my litmus test of heterodox economists is their ability to get jobs at major graduate schools. Marxist and Institutionalist economists are heterodox economists; those on the above list are not. The reality is that, when it comes to content, modern economics is open to new ideas. (I'm not saying totally open, but I am saying at least begrudgingly open.) There are disagreements about content, and about how consistent with general equilibrium theory models should be, but in terms of content, there is significant flexibility, especially at the cutting edge.

THE CENTRAL ATTRIBUTE OF MODERN ECONOMICS

If content does not define modern economics, what does? It is method. The same modern economics that is enormously broad in its acceptance of various assumptions and content is extremely narrow when it comes to method. As Solow (1997) spells out, and as Niehans (1990) emphasizes, *the modeling*

approach to problems is the central element of modern economics. Solow
writes:

> Today, if you ask a mainstream economist a question about almost any aspect of
> economic life, the response will be: suppose we model that situation and see what
> happens. . . . There are thousands of examples; the point is that modern main-
> stream economics consists of little else but examples of this process. (p. 43)

Modeling is not seen as an end in itself; there is a continual discussion of
the need to empirically test, and the formal modeling is undertaken in large
part to make the models empirically testable, and applicable to policy, with
formal statistical techniques.

Given the changes in economics, the "study of the allocation of scarce resources" definition of economics no longer describes what economists do. A
better definition would be "The study of the economy and economic policies
through empirically testable models." An alternative definition comes from
Keynes: "Economics is the science of thinking in terms of models joined to
the art of choosing models which are relevant to the contemporary world."
The point of these new definitions is that they do not consider content; they
consider the approach used. Modern economics is economics of the model.

A MODEL FOR EVERY PURPOSE

To say that modern economics follows a modeling approach is not to say that
other periods did not use models. Economists have always used models. But
there is a distinction in how the models are used. To see the distinction
between modern economists' use of models and earlier economists', it is useful to distinguish between pure theory models and applied policy models.
Formal modeling has always been the essence of pure theory of economics—
the metaphysics, or science, depending on one's view. For example, Quesnay,
Ricardo, Cournot, and Walras all simplified their views to develop a theoretical model. Modern pure theory has evolved from the general equilibrium theory
of Walras to the general equilibrium of Arrow/Debreu, but the modeling approach has not changed. These pure theory models are highly formal and
mathematically deep. But such formal models are not the type of models that
the large proportion of economists deal with.

It is in applied policy where modern economics differs from earlier economics. In previous time periods, economists such as Smith or Marshall kept
the theory in the back of their minds, and thought about the policy problem as
an art. Their models were kept in the background, and reasonableness—critical thought—was emphasized in applying the models. Applied policy belonged

in what J.N. Keynes (1897) called the art of economics. In the art of economics the pure theory model served as a backdrop, but one approached problems in an informal way. Formal empirical testing of such loose models was impossible, but one could easily include non-quantifiable variables and sensibilities in one's policy consideration.

In modern economics that has changed. There is no art of economics in which policy problems are addressed in an informal manner. Modern applied policy models must be specified in a way that can be directly empirically tested, at least in principle. While such models are informal by mathematical standards, they are formal by artistic standards, which is why some observers call modern economics formalist.

Ironically, the modern modeling approach grew out of the Keynesian macroeconomics of the 1930s and Marshall's practical policy approach to problems. It is a blend of the Keynesian and Marshallian visions of economics with the twist that the models are specified in such a way that they are subject to econometric testing. But, in specifying the models so that they are subject to econometric testing, the current approach fundamentally alters the Marshallian approach to policy. The simplified models are moved up to center stage, and the judgment, embodying the blending of the assumptions kept in the back of one's mind which lead to the model's results, is moved to a side stage.

Another aspect of modern applied policy modeling is that, with the exception of work in computable general equilibrium, these models pay almost no heed to consistency with general equilibrium theory. New work in micro emphasizes the development of a variety of practical models, such as the asymmetric pricing model, that are relevant for specific problems, but make no claim that, and give little thought to whether, they are general-equilibrium consistent. Modern applied microeconomics consists of a collection of models with a model for every purpose.

Practical models were not always divorced from pure theory models. In the 1950s and 1960s, it was hoped that practical models would be guided by general equilibrium theory. Thus, when Arrow/Debreu proved the existence of a general equilibrium in 1957, there was hope that the pure science of economics would progress in tandem with the practical application of that science. By the 1970s economists recognized that the Arrow/Debreu general equilibrium work was not going to get to the promised land. That recognition freed economists to deal with practical policy models that were inconsistent with general equilibrium theory.

In my view that recognition accounts for the developments of new growth theory, new trade theory, and other partial equilibrium models that are inconsistent with formal general equilibrium models. They are practical models, which can be loosely tested empirically, and which shed some light on issues.

Shedding some light on a problem is all that the practical track of modern economics requires. Solow (1997) calls this approach "loose fitting positivism." The difference in view can be seen in the change in approach to increasing returns. Whereas in 1939, when the general equilibrium hope was still alive, Hicks commented that assuming increasing returns could lead to the "wreckage of the greater part of general equilibrium theory" (1939, p. 84), in the 1980s and '90s Paul Krugman, and other "new trade," "industrialization," and "growth," theorists proceed as if it is not even an issue. They simply assume away the problems that multiple equilibria and increasing returns raise.

Whereas in micro the evolution has been toward a grab bag of models, the evolution in macro has been different. Modern macro started in the 1940s as a grab bag of *ad hoc* models inconsistent with general equilibrium theory. Throughout the 1950s and 1960s macroeconomics was the essence of pragmatic eclectic modeling. Macro models focused on consumption functions and quantity theories, based on general aggregate relationships, dominated the field. In these models there was no demand for micro foundations.

That state of affairs was challenged by the New Classical revolution, which argued that Keynesian economics needed micro foundations, and had to be consistent with general equilibrium. In the 1980s New Classical economics had a brief day in the sun by adding far-sighted rationality to existing macro models, and justifying that addition with a call for consistency with general equilibrium assumptions. In my view it succeeded in becoming important primarily because it offered relatively easy modeling criteria that led to numerous papers and theses. Its applicability was always in doubt.

By the early 1990s, the New Classical revolution had played itself out; most economists recognized that general equilibrium could not be applied directly to the economy. New Keynesian models incorporated far-sighted rationality but they were primarily partial equilibrium models. Neither New Classical nor New Keynesian models were especially insightful and, in the 1990s, the theoretical focus of attention in macro shifted to growth. Practical and macro modeling was returned to the real-world practitioners and applied macroeconomics returned to pragmatic, *ad hoc* modeling.

PROBLEMS WITH MODERN APPLIED ECONOMICS

In many ways the modern movement to applied modeling is laudable. It is empirical and is an attempt to avoid the pontificating which characterized earlier periods. Modern applied modeling looks to the empirical evidence through models. But it also has problems. Since the connection with general equilibrium theory has been eliminated, there is no theoretical core that limits assumptions. New Classicals criticized the lack of a theoretical core in

Keynesian macro; that criticism led to its success. Put bluntly, modern applied economics is essentially data mining with some semblance of "scientific empirical testing" added to make it seem less *ad hoc*. Don't misinterpret my argument; there is nothing wrong with data mining; you can find out much about the economy in the data. My point is that when you data mine, you undercut your ability to formally statistically test the results in a formal manner. If the assumptions of the model are *ad hoc*, then the results are *ad hoc*. That doesn't mean that the models can't be informally empirically tested and compared with reality, but the major thrust of modern economics is on formal empirical testing of the models. They avoid the semblance of pontificating, by structuring their models in scientific clothing. Thus, in my view, modern applied economics has serious problems.

The problems are exacerbated by incentives within the profession for publishing; these incentives lead to assumptions for the *ad hoc* pragmatic models often being chosen based on their likelihood of getting published, which requires "nice" results and empirical statistical applicability, rather than being chosen based on their reasonableness. These problems are serious, but they are not the problems of neoClassical economics. In fact, they are problems that developed because modern economics has moved away from the neoClassical assumptions and become more eclectic.

THE BIRTH OF NEW MILLENNIUM ECONOMICS

A theory can be replaced only by another theory; a term can be replaced only by another term. The staying power of the term, neoClassical, can, in many ways, be explained by the absence of an alternative. Unless another term is forthcoming and becomes generally accepted, and used by historians of thought and other observers, the term "neoClassical" will continue forever.

A number of alternative terms have been proposed. Yang and Ng (1994) have proposed "new Classical" to describe modern work. The problems with this are (1) the term has already been used to describe an approach to macro; (2) it is unclear whether modern theory is "Classical" in any meaningful sense; and (3) the use of the "new" classification is shortsighted and leads to long-run confusion. Stanley Brue's term for modern economics, "mathematical economics," doesn't work because (1) it is not descriptive of much of what is done—most policy models use little deep mathematics; (2) it misses the empirical testing aspect of the modeling; and (3) practitioners such as Solow don't like it. The "formalist" classification fails for similar reasons.

Jurg Niehans has come the closest in classifying the modern era when he called modern economics "the era of modeling"(1990). It is descriptive, and acceptable to most practitioners (Solow emphasized the modeling aspect of modern economics in his description). Its problems are that it fails to capture the nature of the modern applied policy modeling, specifically its tendency to simplify in an *ad hoc* manner, and then empirically test. As I stated above, economists have always modeled; what distinguishes approaches is the nature of the modeling. *Ad hoc* modelers, or eclectic modelers, would be more descriptive.

My proposal for what to call modern economics is New Millennium Economics. In doing so I am following Schumpeter's lead in classifying schools by temporal terms. The advantages of doing so are the following: (1) The term fits in with the millennium rage; (2) It is forward looking, and thus does not have to deal with the issue of what economics was from 1930 to 2000; some can see it as a transition period; others can see it as the early beginning of New Millennium economics; (3) It is ideologically neutral; it does not come with the excess baggage of Classical or Keynesian or neo or new terminology (although it will have to be changed when 3000 roles around); and (4) It is easily broken up—there can be an early 21st century and a late 21st century branch.

CONCLUSION

Let me conclude by briefly talking about changes I see occurring in the future. The changes will be driven by developments in theory that allow modern economics to come to grips with the disconnect between their practical *ad hoc* models and their pure theory general equilibrium models. This can be accomplished in two ways. The underlying pure theory can change, or applied policy work can change. Or, as I see it, both can change.

In pure theory there are two complementary directions research is taking. One is the development of a general equilibrium theory that is based on evolutionary game theory, supplemented by experimental economics. This approach "solves" the multiple equilibrium problem by adding an analysis of equilibria selection mechanisms. That work has the potential to change the way we think about general equilibrium theory by providing a richer foundation from which to build practical models.

The other direction is the one complexity theorists take. Their work provides an alternative to a general equilibrium foundation. In the complexity approach, one takes the position that something so complex as the aggregate economy cannot have formal analytic foundations; hence our understanding of it must proceed through alternative means. In complex systems, order spontaneously develops as patterns emerge. Simplicity of complex systems is to be found in the study of dynamics and iterative processes, not in structural simplicity. In the complexity approach everything is data mining, but it is a highly sophisticated data mining done under specific rules—rules that are just now developing. It is still a modeling approach, but it is done with computer simulations.[9] The ever-falling costs of computing will push this approach forward in the 21st century.

The other change that I see occurring is in how one tests practical models, and in how one decides on assumptions. Here I see experimental economics as playing a central role. Experimental economics offers a way of choosing among various equilibria that result from game-theoretic models. I believe it is because of the hope provided by experimental economics that game theory is succeeding now whereas before it did not. Thus, I regard the experimental economics movement as an important development in modern economics. Experimental economics provides a whole new way of testing and applying economic models. Because it does, experimental economics will grow significantly and be an important pillar of 21st century economics. Although currently, by my graduate school standards, experimental economics is not yet mainstream, I predict it soon will be.[10]

While I think there will be many changes in economics over the coming century, pragmatic modeling, the major focus of what economists do, is here to stay; it will be the hallmark of New Millennium Economics. Current economics is institutionally stable; it can get enough funding to keep its practitioners doing what they are doing. There will be an evolution, not a revolution. It was in thinking about how to tell the story of that evolution that I came to the conclusion that the term, neoClassical, must be pronounced dead. Modern economics is fundamentally different from neoClassical economics, and if we are to tell the story of modern economics effectively, we must have a term for modern economics that makes that point.

NOTES

*   There was a bug—the y2k bug—that came along at the turn of the millennium and bit otherwise sane people, leading them to pontificate about grand issues. Individuals, such as me, who have a natural proclivity to pontificate were especially susceptible, so I ask your forbearance at the beginning; this chapter was written under the influence.

1.   Actually, it is not clear to me that I have the power to do so, but since my term is almost over, I will assume that before impeachment proceedings can be completed, I will be out of office.

2.   Schumpeter (1954) is an exception. He deals with the issue in his discussion of the problems of periodization.

3.   It might be argued by a cynic that that ambiguity is precisely the image the terms are meant to bring forth.

4.   As I will discuss below in my treatment of the history of the neoClassical classification, that intertemporal role is questionable too.

5.   Schumpeter considers the issue of classification of Classical economics carefully. In a footnote (p. 379) he remarks that there were three uses of the term Classical. (Elizabeth Schumpeter, who edited the book from his notes, states that this section was unfinished.)

6.   See Tony Aspromourgos (1986) for a discussion. See also Susan Fayazmanesh (1998).

7. For example, in his methodological postcript he writes "the besetting methodological vice of neoClassical economics was the illegitimate use of microstatic theories" (p. 701).
8. Schumpeter (1954) writes: "Multiple equilibria are not necessarily useless, but from the standpoint of any exact science the existence of a uniquely determined equilibrium is, of course, of the utmost importance, even if proof has to be purchased at the price of very restrictive assumptions; without any possibility of proving the existence of (a) uniquely determined equilibrium—or at all events, of a small number of possible equilibria—at however high a level of abstraction, a field of phenomena is really a chaos that is not under analytical control."
9. One individual stands out at the center of both approaches: John von Neumann. His 1928 paper, and his 1944 book with Oskar Morgenstern on game theory, pointed the way to expanding general equilibrium via game theory; his work on artificial life and computers is at the foundation of the complexity approach to economics.
10. The reason experimental economics hasn't become mainstream is that the training required to do it well is so fundamentally different from the training for doing standard deductive economics. This means that integrating it into the curriculum is not a marginal process; it is a jump process.

12. New Millennium Economics in 2050: How Did It Get This Way, and What Way is It?*

New Millennium economics evolved out of neoClassical economics over the last 100 years. The pace of change increased over time and in the first half of the 21st century, the economics profession has changed as much, or more, than it did in the last half of the 20th century. The changes occurred both because of the internal tensions in the profession in the second part of the 20th century and because of technological changes that affected both the research methods of economics and the structure of higher education generally. In this chapter I consider that evolution. I will organize my discussion in two sections: the first focusing on changes in the structure of economic education; the second focusing on changes in the content of what economists do.

FROM 2000–2050: CHANGES IN THE STRUCTURE OF GRADUATE ECONOMIC EDUCATION

Although the number of economics graduate students expanded substantially in the 1950s and 1960s, the fundamental structure of graduate economics education did not change much at all in the second half of the 20th century. However, the structure of economics education has undergone profound changes in the 50 years since 2000.

THE DECLINE OF IMPORTANCE OF GEOGRAPHIC PLACE: THE RISE OF THE VIRTUAL UNIVERSITY

The first major change that occurred is external to economics: in 2000, "geographic place" was still central to education. By 2050, geographic place has become far less important; "brand" is far more important. Going to university or college used to mean going to a particular geographic place; for a few of the top colleges and universities this is still the case, but for a majority of students it no longer means that. Virtual universities, collections of scholars from around the world who have combined into an accredited program of study in a particular field, have grown enormously, and have significantly displaced many geographically-based programs.[1]

The burgeoning growth of these virtual universities has led to an increased importance of accrediting agencies; the highest-level accrediting group, the International University Accreditation Association (IUAA), was created by an international consortium of universities. Many other alternative accreditation groups exist and almost all of the 25,000 virtual universities worldwide are accredited by some agency. However, the IUAA is predominant. My discussion of structure deals only with the IUAA-accredited institutions.

The development of these virtual universities was driven by developments in information and communications technology. Complete virtual classes, where each student is virtually recreated in an interactive classroom setting regardless of where the students actually are, have replaced in-person classes as they were conducted even in the opening years of the 21st century.[2] Entrance into a typical university graduate program in economics now allows students a choice of 30 virtual discussion groups, 40 virtual classes, and 40 virtual seminars in economics.

With the enormous expansion of virtual universities has come a narrowing in the number of IUAA-accredited schools, which has meant a significant shakeup in structure for graduate economics programs. Of the approximately 100 US universities granting Ph.D.s in economics in 2000, only 20 remain as IUAA-accredited stand-alone options, and even these stand-alone universities have entered into virtual partnerships that increase course options for their students. The others have merged into consortiums and the degrees they give are consortium degrees. Some of these consortiums are highly competitive; at present, three of the ten top-ranked schools in composite rankings of economic programs are consortium schools. The consortiums that developed from existing non-profit universities still have their geographic homes where students can live if they choose, but a graduate student accepted into a "virtual university" can reside at any of the 20 or so locations that comprise the physical "university"—or can reside at none of them. Students attending these virtual universities are generally geographic nomads, residing at two or three individual schools during their studies to work with specific mentors.

A CHANGE IN THE GEOGRAPHIC CENTER OF GRAVITY OF ECONOMICS

This rise of virtual universities has meant a de-Americanization of graduate schools in general and of graduate economics programs in specific. Of course, the geographic center of the economics profession is harder to measure than it was back in 2000, since most of the foreign programs have US components and, indeed, while most of the IUAA-accredited on-line universities are in large part foreign-based, all have US schools in the consortium. However, the United States was clearly the center of the economics profession in 2000, but in 2050, it is far less important as a center. In 2000, the American Economic Association was the premier economics organization in the world; today, of course, it is the International Economics Association; the AEA is one of many regional organizations.

In 2050, the economics profession has three competing centers: one in Europe, one in the United States, and one in Asia. The seeds of the end of American dominance of the economics profession were sown back in the late 20th century when the student body of top economics programs became heavily dominated by foreign students. Throughout the early 21st century, the majority of these top foreign-born economists stayed in the United States. But when the Great Depression of 2025 struck, hurting the US economy more than it hurt the rest of the world, and geographic units of virtual universities in their countries of origin made lucrative offers to these economists to return home, many moved back, and they took top journals and reputations with them.

INCREASED SPECIALIZATION IN ECONOMICS TRAINING

In the 1990s and early 2000s, "graduate work in economics" was rather unidimensional. Becoming "an economist" meant studying economics at a graduate program in economics, and the majority of graduate programs, and all the top-ranked schools, were quite homogeneous. In the first years of graduate school, in particular, everyone learned essentially the same set of models, the same approaches.

Since then, the field of economics has discovered, or rediscovered, Adam Smith's division of labor and need for specialization. In 2050, the majority of consortiums granting economics-related degrees have multiple tracks. People no longer become generic economists; instead they are clearly designated as specialists in public finance, health care, macro forecasting, forensic economics, industrial relations, and other areas. To be sure, graduate study in economics still starts with one semester of general core courses: one in micro, one in complex systems analysis, and one in statistics. However, these courses are not technical courses, as they were in the 1990s and early 2000s; they are survey courses given to acquaint students with the broad field of economics. Immediately after these courses, students begin specialized study in one, or sometimes two, areas of specialty. Each of these areas of specialty, or tracks, has its own set of required courses and knowledge. The track that is most equivalent to the program students followed in their first two years in the 1990s and early 2000s is the economic theory track. This track is now a specialty track for those few going on in theory and its membership is very small; its requirements are very difficult; and since few jobs are available for its graduates, most of them have to spend some years in low-paid postdoctoral work hoping to find one of the few theoretical research positions available.

One of the tracks is a "general economics" track, which primarily serves to prepare individuals to teach economics principles to undergraduates, which remains one of economists' most important jobs. This track primarily gives an overview of various subfields rather than going deeply into the technical aspects. General-track economists often do work in another specialty area as well. The liberal arts research college consortium, which started granting Ph.D.s in 2020 and has grown enormously in the last 30 years, is the primary provider of degrees in this track. Almost no graduates of other programs go on to undergraduate teaching; most go on into business and government.

REDEFINITION OF BOUNDARIES

This increased specialization has been accompanied by a redefinition of boundaries of graduate economics programs within institutions. In the 1990s, firm institutional boundaries existed between public policy schools, arts and sciences schools, engineering schools, business schools, law schools, and medical schools. By 2050, these boundaries have broken down. Most of the existing specialties that comprise economics evolved out of a combination of schools or programs within schools. For example, a person studying health economics now will go to a health economics program that evolved out of a combination of economics programs, medical school programs, and public policy school programs. A person studying macroeconomics now will study jointly with engineering complex systems schools and an economics program. In fact, one might say that in 2050 there are no longer "economists," but, instead, health economists, statistical specialists, simulations experts who focus on economic issues, public finance specialists, and so on.

The changing of the boundaries did not come easily and involved much infighting. The evolution of the changes is worth recounting. In the closing decades of the 20th century, graduate economics programs provided the professors to teach in public policy and business schools. As those programs grew, and become more specialized and rigorous, these schools became self-replicating. They hired their own Ph.D. graduates to teach in their programs, developed their own journals, and split off from economics *per se*.

Public policy schools in particular developed their own brand of economics, which grew in importance throughout the first part of the 21st century. By about 2020 they had become the major suppliers of economists not only to their own programs but to other programs as well, as traditional graduate programs in economics shrank in size or merged into virtual universities. With the Liberal Arts Research Consortium siphoning off many of the students who were planning to go into undergraduate teaching, the old-style economics graduate programs found they had lost much of their clientele. The depression of 2025 hit the economics graduate programs hard and many were simply closed; those that continued did so by becoming sub-components of the larger public policy consortiums. The individual tracks in economics developed as part of this consolidation.

CHANGES IN THE CONTENT OF ECONOMICS

Let me now turn to changes in the content of economics—changes in what graduate students in economics are taught as opposed to changes in the structure of the institutions within which they are taught. To set the stage for how economics has changed in the first half of the 21st century, it is useful to begin by thinking back to the evolution of economics in the second half of the 20th century.

Twentieth-century economics generally was called neoClassical economics, although the term does not do justice to the transformation of economics during that century. For example, as Robert Solow pointed out, back in the 1940s economics was basically a descriptive, institutional subject for a "gentleman scholar."[3] The textbooks of the time were "civilized" and discursive—a melding of insights, numerical examples, and classifications. They had sensible discussions of economic policy and serious looks at recent history as it would be seen by an economist. Formal analysis was minimized. This approach made economics the domain of intuitive economists. It was a domain that some people found too hard and some found too easy. Keynes (1924) summed up the difficulty in this approach in his well-known pronouncement that economics requires a mixture of common sense and analytic ability that is quite uncommon.[4]

By 2000, the economics profession had changed fundamentally, and in the history of thought we use 2000 as the end of the neoClassical era and the beginning of the New Millennium Era.[5] Solow (1997, p. 41) defined the economics of the 1990s as "a collection of analytical tools to be applied quite directly to observable situations." The shift in emphasis from the 1940s to the 1990s did not occur suddenly; it occurred slowly over the period as older economists retired and younger ones came in.

What distinguished the economics of the late 1990s was not formalism *per se*. While the economic models of the 1990s often contained a hearty dose of mathematics, the mathematics itself was almost never deep. Moreover, relatively few economists worked on formal theory at the turn of the century. Instead, the key component of the economics in the late 1990s was "model-building." In graduate schools, students didn't learn much about actual institutions or problems; instead, they all learned the same basic set of analytic models, which they then applied directly to reality.

Undergraduate teaching was somewhat different, reflecting easier models, and in the 1990s there was a significant tension between the two, with a large proportion of the graduate students having a relatively weak background in undergraduate economics. Solow attributed the spread of model-building to several factors: the problems the older discursive approach had with maintaining objectivity, the demand of policymakers for quantitative answers, and the fact that even the primitive computers of that time had produced an increased availability of data and the greater ease of analyzing that data.

New Millennium economists still use models, but they are quite different models from the deductive models of the 1990s that Solow describes. Modern models are more like weather models in the late 1990s. These modern models come to many of the same conclusions as the old models; economists still believe price incentives are important, and that markets solve coordination problems, but those beliefs are not held with the almost religious conviction with which they were held in the neoClassical era. Specifically, New Millennium economics does not base policy on the neoClassical welfare theorems, which were part of its broader "right price" view of policy. That view of policy has been replaced by our current "right institutions" view of policy.[6] This is not to say that the optimal rationing ideas found in the welfare theorems are not still used; they are. It is only to say that they are used as a subcomponent of a broader institutional policy analysis. They provide insight given institutions, not about institutions.

THE FALL OF LOOSE-FITTING POSITIVISM AND THE RISE OF PRAGMATISM

At the end of the 20th century, Solow (1997) called the methodology underlying the policy-oriented models "loose-fitting positivism." By that he meant that economists believed that they were taking models that in some sense were consistent with "standard" economic principles, and "testing" the validity of those models empirically. Through the 1990s, economic researchers typically started with a set of principles: for example, utility-maximizing by consumers and profit-maximizing for firms, far-sighted individual rationality, and a belief in equilibrium, which meant that, structurally, individuals' decisions in the models fit reasonably well together. These principles were probably best embodied in Arrow and Debreu's work (1954; Debreu, 1957). During the second half of the 1900s, they first became comprehensively embedded in microeconomic models, and then, as Keynesian economics declined and New Classical macroeconomics became dominant in the 1980s, they spread to macroeconomics as well. By the late 20th century, these principles formed the core of economists' vision of reality, in the sense that all economic models were built on these principles, or around variations of these principles like assumptions of bounded rationality or imperfect information.[7]

Thus, in the 1990s, economists saw the models that were deduced from first principles as providing a theoretical foundation for their work. However, in the closing decades of the 20th century, it became clear that the models actually being used for policy purposes were diverging from the underlying formal general equilibrium models at their core. With some justice, the policy models became viewed as more and more *ad hoc*. Instead of being closely tied to underlying general equilibrium core models, policy models embodied selectively chosen empirical regularities and principles. As a result, controversy arose over how to interpret policy models. To critics, the policy models were seen as "data mining," where the analytics provided scientific cover for the desired policy conclusions of the authors, rather than objective analysis leading to reliable results.[8] One article of the time referred to then-current empirical work as a "zero-communication informational equilibrium," in which "the researcher has the motive and opportunity to present his results selectively, and the reader, knowing this, imputes a low or zero signal-to-noise ratio to the reported results" (Cooley and Leroy, 1981, p. 826).

The critics could point to some evidence for their distrust of empirical work. The editors of the *Journal of Money, Banking and Credit* found that even when they had requested the data from authors (which was almost never done at that time, because of the primitive state of computing power), they could not replicate the results of the studies (Dewald *et al.,* 1986). Remember, this was straightforward replication, not even taking into account whether the particular *ad hoc* model chosen by the author was especially appropriate! McCloskey and Ziliak (1996) found that statistical inference was incorrectly used in a large majority of articles in the *American Economic Review*, the premier journal of the period. Little wonder that in a 1997 survey of economists, 95 percent of the respondents were at least somewhat skeptical of empirical work (Mayer, 1997). These problems led to changes in the way data analysis was conducted and reported.

In 2050, economists no longer believe that a set of canonical principles will lead to a single model that is then tested in empirical work. Today, most of the simulation models that form the core of what students are taught deviate from the old-style canonical principles in some way or another. In 2050, the belief of economists in derived analytical models has given way to a belief that the underlying reality is too complex to be understood with these sorts of models.

Economists in 2050 do empirical work in a wider variety of ways than they did at the turn of the millennium. They both create data and analyze it. Experimental economics is now an extremely important way of creating data; interestingly, it only began in the late 20th century.[9] Economists today also use natural experiments and randomized field trials to create data much more than they did formerly. Finally, New Millennium economists tease information out of data sets with complex statistical programs that automatically report correlations under multiple specifications and undertake standard robustness tests of those correlations. Such statistical analysis is routinely done with all data sets. New Millennium economists do not believe that they are testing a particular model that was deduced from first principles; instead they are simply looking for possibly exploitable patterns in the data. The loose-fitting positivism of 50 years ago has changed to a loose-fitting pragmatism.

THE RISE OF COMPLEXITY SCIENCE

The movement of economists away from deductive principles was based on an evolving belief that complexity science is the appropriate domain for economics. This belief followed the rise of complexity science within the scientific community generally and the growing understanding that complex systems are not beyond scientific analysis.

New Millennium economics divides phenomena into those which are susceptible to what might be called "structural simplification," in which models with linear dynamics and unique analytic solutions are used, and those susceptible to "replicative process simplification" in which data are simplified into non-linear dynamic models with no unique analytic solution.[10] In the 1990s, structural simplification existed as the only scientific approach. If economics was unsusceptible to structural simplification it was beyond science; not surprisingly, economics of the time followed a structural simplification program. The structural simplification research program held that simplicity was to be found in structural models. To keep those models tractable, researchers typically had to assume simple (often linear) dynamics and relatively simple structural equations, and had to adhere to the first principles of maximizing behavior, rationality, equilibrium, and so on.

The replicative process research program, also known as the complexity approach, follows a different pattern. Instead of beginning from certain principles and assuming linear dynamics, a wide variety of organizing principles and dynamics became conceivable. The 1990s saw the beginning of complexity science. By 2020, complexity science had developed to the point where most scientists accepted the view that the old-style research path worked well for structurally simple systems, but the complexity path was necessary for complex systems. By 2030, most economic researchers believed that the economy was a complex system that belonged within complexity science.

Let me mention just one change that characterizes the difference in approach. In the 1990s, an active research program in economics looked for microeconomic foundations on which to build macroeconomic theories. The methodology held that if aggregate macroeconomic results were to be trusted, they had to be derived from microfoundations that were built on rationality, maximizing behavior. The acceptance that economics was a complex system ended that belief; now we believe that microfoundations are contextual, and that the order we observe in complex systems arises spontaneously. Complexity science finds the temporary pattern in complex systems.

Complexity science has a less ambitious agenda than did the old standard science. It does not search for general results that hold for all times; instead, it searches for temporary patterns that develop spontaneously in complex systems. Equilibrium may sometimes occur, or it may not. Complex systems are always evolving and expanding with new complex patterns emerging, making all patterns of complex systems potentially temporary.

THE INCREASE IN COMPUTATIONAL POWER

Complexity science was able to develop in the 1990s because the advances in computer technology, which even in the clunky technology of that time (they still used keyboards!) had begun to allow meaningful analysis that were more and more complex. The implications of this change resonated throughout economics. For example, as late as the opening decade of the 21st century, supply and demand graphs were still the central organizing feature of economics, and the workhorses of economic pedagogy. Of course, in 2050, supply and demand graphs are seldom used explicitly. Instead, the development in computer power has allowed use of on-line dynamic simulations in which students play scenarios.

The huge drop in the relative costs of computation has also had a dramatic effect on the way in which applied and theoretical economics is done. In the 1990s and sometimes in the early 2000s, one pictured an economic policy analyst sitting with a pen and paper working with an analytic model—then going to the computer to test it. In 2050, the picture of an economist is of a person sitting at the computer doing analytic and data analysis simultaneously, relying on computer programs that take data, analyze it, and suggest eight or ten alternative models that fit it. Of course, the modern approach poses issues of its own, as discussed in the "Symposium on the Robustness of Simulation Models" in the Summer 2048 issue of the journal in which an earlier version of this chapter appeared, but the problems are different in kind from the problems that arose a half-century ago.

It may be instructive to review how the change came about. Decreased costs of computation lowered the cost to understanding via computer brawn, and thereby reduced the relative value of the analytic deductive approach to understanding used in the 20th century.[11] Economic theory no longer needed to be built from a deep bedrock of fundamental results; instead it could be based on computer-aided observation and search for patterns. In the 1990s and early 2000s, the usual proof of a proposition in economics relied little on previously observed economic patterns and instead relied on a combination of structural assumptions and existing mathematical theorems; in New Millennium economics, "proofs" in economics rely much more heavily on empirically determined economic patterns that have developed through simulation work, experimental work, and economic modeling built on generally-accepted observed patterns. What Charles Peirce, the 19th century philosopher, called "abduction" replaced deduction.

Of course, characteristics like rationality and maximizing behavior have not disappeared from economic analysis, but their extent and direction now need to be observed, not assumed. For example, the degree of rationality, the extent of information, and the consistency of beliefs over time and in the face of various situations are all among the empirical regularities determined in behavioral economics rather than based on assumptions. Purposeful action is still a hallmark of economic models, but what is "purposeful" is now developed endogenously, based on observations of actual behavior; again, it is not exogenously assumed. Likewise, equilibrium is a pattern that can occur and may even last for a time, but it is never assumed. Instead, it is always temporary, part of a wider "complex adaptive system" in which new patterns are constantly emerging.[12]

CHANGE IN THEORETICAL AND APPLIED MODELS

Let me put these changes in the content of economics into perspective by briefly considering some early harbingers of the complexity approach around the turn of the century. The first paper I want to consider is a turn-of-the-century largely theoretical paper written by Peter Howitt and Robert Clower (2000).[13] They began with a number of observations, which they translated into a set of rules. Then, they built a theoretical simulation model based on these rules, and studied the self-organizing patterns that emerged from the model. Put another way, they "grew" their economic model rather than assuming it. In their simulation model, all economic organization, including equilibrium (or the lack of it) and markets themselves, are outcomes following from the rules about transactions costs, not from assumptions.

An early example of the use of complexity approach in applied economic work can be seen in the work of Quirmbach (1993) who evaluated the tradeoff between the degree of competition and the level of investment. In the standard view of the 1990s, if future competition was expected to be very intense, then the current levels of investment in R&D might be lower than socially desirable. Quirmbach computed hundreds of cases of different market structures, implying differing degrees of competition, and found a robust pattern that suggested that allowing collusion or monopoly to stimulate the appropriate level of R&D was usually a poor idea from a social welfare perspective. The interest here is not the result, but the method. His result was not a "theorem" in the traditional sense of economic theory, but it was a valuable policy result, because the robustness of his findings was unsuspected. As computational costs dropped, this pattern-search approach to policy expanded and became the dominant method of policy analysis. It substantially reduced the need for a deductive foundation and thereby played a role in the changing structure of economics graduate education discussed above.

Initially, the economics profession fought the computer approach with the vehemence that Luddites of the 19th century and the linotype operators of the 20th century fought technical change in their occupations. Because of deductive economists' structural control of the profession in the early 21st century, initially this fight was highly successful, but, eventually, the new technology won and computation has replaced deduction as the primary workhorse of applied and theoretical economics.

CONCLUSION

Robert Solow (1997) concluded his summary of the state of economics near the end of the 20th century with a paraphrase of Oscar Wilde's description of a fox hunt—"the unspeakable in pursuit of the inedible"—by saying that perhaps economics was an example of "the overeducated in pursuit of the unknowable." Despite the ongoing controversies in the field of economics today, New Millennium economists are far more comfortable with what they do after the changes in the structure and content of economics over the last half–century.

The better feeling about being overeducated has occurred because of the change in the structure of economics. The view that economists were overeducated followed in large part from the approach to economic training in the 1990s, in which all students went through the same extensive training—and inevitably, ended up using relatively little of it in their later professional work. New Millennium economic training is much more individually focused, with the training of students concentrating on those aspects of knowledge more relevant for their proposed field.

Rather than bounding after the unknowable, and trying to analytically deduce models that hold for all times, economics has reduced its search to what it believes is knowable. New Millennium economists search for patterns in data, try to find temporary models that fit the patterns, and study the changing nature of those patterns as institutions change.

In some ways, the economics profession has come full circle back to the more descriptive and institutional approach that was common a full century ago, in the middle of the 20th century. The underlying mathematical structure of models and computational techniques that economists use in 2050 is, of course, much more complicated, but most economists are being trained to use these tools, not to derive them. This frees the training of graduate students to focus on what textbooks of the 1940s focused on—melding together insights, numerical examples, classification, and simulations to arrive at sensible discussions of policy—and allows me to describe economics in 2050 as the "appropriately educated in search of the knowable."

NOTES

*   The title of this chapter is adapted from an article by Robert Solow (1997), a famous economist of the late 20th century. I would like to thank journal editors for helpful comments on an earlier version of this chapter. I also would like to explain the referencing mechanism I am using (putting authors, dates, and a bibliography within the chapter), which I am sure looks strange to you. This is the referencing system they used at the turn of the century. For all pre–2010 references, I thought it would be useful to maintain that system to give you an idea of the practices then. For supporting statements on all post-2010 references I use the Network Standard Referencing System. Simply highlight the text you are interested in and use your Inquire command to access my references, my supporting arguments, and to carry our a complete literature search in this area, with the findings prioritized by the IAB Weighting System. It is for that same reason that I give an e-mail address, which was a system of communication used before direct access was developed.

1.   At the turn of the century most professors were associated with only one university whereas today they are associated with as many as 20 virtual universities, drawing a portion of their salary from each.

2.   The development of virtual transport in 2022, which made it almost impossible to distinguish "being there" from "virtually being there," had a devastating effect on the transportation industry and is believed by many to be an important cause of the depression of 2025.

3.   This discussion is based on Robert Solow's 1997 essay.

4.   The precise quotation is the following: "The study of economics does not seem to require any specialized gifts of an unusually high order. Is it not, intellectually regarded, a very

easy subject compared with the higher branches of philosophy and pure science. Yet good, or even competent, economists are the rarest of birds. An easy subject at which very few excel!" (Keynes, 1924, pp. 321–22).

5. For a discussion of the transformation and for an early use of the term "New Millennium Economics" see the previous chapter.

6. For an early discussion of New Millennium policy issues see Brock and Colander (2000).

7. For a discussion of these key assumptions in the mindset of economists in the later 1990s, see Kreps (1997).

8. Some prominent critics in the 1980s and 1990s included Tom Mayer (1993a, 1997), Deirdre McCloskey (1985), and Edward Leamer (1983), who captured much of this concern in their writings.

9. Vernon Smith and Charles Plott did not win their Nobel Prizes for that work until 2006.

10. Zipf's Law and Per Bak's scaling Law are early examples of the replicative process simplification. For a further discussion of replicative process simplifications see Brock (2000).

11. For an early discussion of this pattern, see Judd (1998).

12. The complexity approach has significant historical precedence. For a discussion of this see Colander (2000)

13. The underlying model in C+ of this paper is still kept on the web at <http://www.econ.ohiostate.edu/howitt> as a museum piece.

Bibliography

Adams, W., J.W. Brock and N. Obst (1991), "Pareto Optimality and Antitrust Policy: The Old Chicago and the New Learning," *Southern Economic Journal*, 58 (1): 1–4.

Arrow, K and G. Debreu (1954), "Existence of an Equilibrium for A Competitive Economy," *Econometrica*, July, 22: 265–90.

Arthur, W.B., S. Durlauf and D. Lane (eds) (1997), *The Economy as an Evolving Complex System II*, Reading, MA: Addison Wesley.

Aslanbeigui, N. and V. Montecinos (1998), "Foreign Students in US Doctoral Programs," *Journal of Economic Perspectives*, 12(3): 171–82.

Aspromourgos, T. (1986), "On the Origin of the Term 'NeoClassical,'" *Cambridge Journal of Economics*, 10 (30): 265–70.

Backhouse, R. (1985), *A History of Modern Economic Analysis*, New York: Basil Blackwell.

Barro, R. (1996), *Getting it Right*, Cambridge, MA: MIT Press.

Basmann, R.L. (1972), "The Brookings Quarterly Econometric Model: Science or Number Mysticism?" and "Arguments and Evidence in the Brookings-S.S.R.C. Philosophy of Econometrics," respectively chapters 1 and 3 in K. Brunner (ed.), *Problems and Issues in Current Econometric Practice*, OH: College of Administrative Science, Ohio State University.

Bennett, A. (1996), "Economists + Meeting = A Zillion Causes and Effects," in D. Colander and J. Gamber (eds), *Case Studies in Macroeconomics*, pp. 39–42, Burr Ridge, IL: Maxi Press/Irwin.

Blaug, M. (1980), *The Methodology of Economics,* Cambridge: Cambridge University Press.

_____ (1985), *Economic Theory in Retrospect*, New York: Cambridge University Press.

_____ (1998), "The Formalist Revolution or What Happened to Orthodox Economics After World War II," *98/10 Discussion Paper in Economics*, October, University of Exeter.

Bodkin, R.G., L.R. Klein and K. Marwah (1991), A *History of Macroeconometric Model-Building,* Aldershot, UK: Edward Elgar.

Boland, L. (1991), "Positivism in Economics and Accounting," manuscript, Simon Fraser University.

Brock, W. (2000), "Some Santa Fe Scenery" in D. Colander (ed.), *The Complexity Vision and the Teaching of Economics*, Aldershot: Edward Elgar.

_____ and D. Colander (2000), "Complexity and Policy" in D. Colander (ed.),*The Complexity Vision and the Teaching of Economics*, Aldershot, UK: Edward Elgar.

Brue, S.L. (1994), *The Evolution of Economic Thought*, 5th ed., New York: Dryden Press.

Colander, D. (1984), "Was Keynes a Keynesian or a Lernerian?," *Journal of Economic Literature* (December): 1572–75.

_____ (1991a), "The Best as the Enemy of the Good" in D. Colander, *Why Aren't Economists as Important as Garbagemen? Essays on the State of Economics*, Armonk, NY: M.E. Sharpe, Inc., pp. 31–7.

_____ (1991b), *Why Aren't Economists as Important as Garbagemen? Essays on the State of Economics,* Armonk, NY: M.E. Sharpe, Inc.

_____ (1995), "The Stories We Tell: A Reconsideration of AS/AD Analysis," *Journal of Economic Perspectives,* 9: 169–88.

_____ (ed.) (1996), *Post Walrasian Economics,* New York: Cambridge University Press.

_____ (1998), *Economics*, Burr Ridge, IL: Irwin-McGraw Hill.

_____ (ed.) (2000), *Complexity and the History of Economic Thought*, London: Routledge.

_____ and R. Brenner (eds) (1992), *Educating Economists*, Ann Arbor: University of Michigan Press.

_____ and D. Daane (1994), T*he Art of Monetary Policy*, Armonk, NY: ME Sharpe.

_____ and A. Klamer (1987), "The Making of an Economist," *Journal of Economic Perspectives,* Fall: 95–111.

_____ and H. Landreth (1994), *History of Economic Thought*, 3rd ed., Boston: Houghton Mifflin Company.

_____ and H. Landreth (eds) (1996), *The Coming of Keynesianism to America,* Aldershot, UK: Edward Elgar Publishers.

Cooley, T. and S. Leroy (1981), "Identification and Estimation of Money Demand," *American Economic Review,* 71: 825–44.

Debreu, G. (1959), *Theory of Value*, New Haven, CT: Yale University Press.

Dewald, W. G., J.G. Thursby and R.G.Anderson (1986), "Replication in Empirical Economics: The Journal of Money, Credit and Banking Project," *American Economic Review*, September: 587–603.

Dornbush, R., S. Fisher and R. Startz (1999), *Macroeconomics,* Burr Ridge, IL: McGraw Hill.

Ekelund, R. Jr. and R. Hebert (1997), *A History of Economic Theory and Method*, 4th ed., New York: McGraw-Hill.

Fayazmanesh, S. (1998), "On Veblen's Coining of the Term 'NeoClassical,'" in S. Fayazmanesh and Marc R. Tool (eds), *Institutionalist Method and Value: Essays in Honour of Paul Dale Bush*, vol. 1, Aldershot, UK: Edward Elgar.

Feldstein, M. (1974), "Social Security, Induced Retirement and Aggregate Capital Accumulation," *Journal of Political Economy* 83(5) : 905–26.

Friedman, M. (1950), "Wesley C. Mitchell as an Economic Theorist," *Journal of Political Economy,* 58 (December): 465–93.

_____ (1952), *Essays in Positive Economics,* Chicago: University of Chicago Press.

_____ (1953), "The Methodology of Positive Economics," in *Essays in Positive Economics*, Chicago: University of Chicago Press.

_____ (1961), *Price Theory: A Provisional Text,* Chicago: University of Chicago Press.

_____ and A.J. Schwartz (1991), "Alternative Approaches to Analyzing Economic Data," *American Economic Review,* 81 (March): 39-49.

Fromm, G. and L.R. Klein (1972), "The Brookings Econometric Model: A Rational Perspective," in K. Brunner (ed.), *Problems and Issues in Current Econometric Practice*, Columbus, OH: College of Administrative Science, Ohio State University.

Hall, R. and J. Taylor (1997), *Macroeconomics*, New York: Norton.

Hammond, D.J. (1991a), "Early Drafts of Friedman's Methodological Essay," manuscript, Winston-Salem, NC: Wake Forest University.

_____ (1991b), "Alfred Marshall's Methodology," *Methodus* 3 (June): 95–101.

_____ (1992), "The Origins of Friedman's Marshallian Analysis," Winston-Salem, NC: Wake Forest University working paper.

Hicks, J.R. (1932), "Marginal Productivity and the Principle of Variation," *Economica*, February.

_____ (1934), "Leon Walras," *Econometrica*, October.

_____ (1939), *Value and Capital,* Oxford: Clarendon.

_____ (1983), *Classics and Moderns* (Collected Essays on Economic Theory, vol. III), Oxford: Basil Blackwell.

Hirsch, A. and N. De Marchi (1990), *Milton Friedman: Economics in Theory and Practice*, Ann Arbor: University of Michigan Press.

Hobson, J.A. (1925), "Neo-Classical Economics in Britain," *Political Science Quarterly*, September.

Howitt, P. and R. Clower (2000), "The Emergence of Economic Organization," Center for Computable Economics Working Paper.

Hutchison, T.W. (1964), *Positive Economics and Policy Objectives,* London: Allen and Unwin.

_____ (1992), *Changing Aims in Economics,* Oxford: Blackwell.

Hutt, W.H. (1979), *The Keynesian Episode: A Reassessment,* Indianapolis, IN: Liberty Press.

Jonsson, P.O. (1995), "On the Economics of Say and Keynes' Interpretation of Say's Law," *Eastern Economic Journal,* 21 (Spring): 147–55.

Judd, K. (1998), *Numerical Methods in Economics*, Cambridge, MA: MIT Press.

Kamarck, A. (1983), *Economics and the Real World,* Philadelphia: University of Pennsylvania Press.

Kennedy, P.E. (2000), "Sinning in the Basement: What are the Rules? The Ten Commandments of Applied Economics," working paper, Simon Fraser University.

Keynes, J.M. (ed.) (1921), "Introduction to Cambridge Economic Handbooks," in D.H. Robertson, *Money*, London and Cambridge: Cambridge Economic Handbooks.

_____ (1924), "Alfred Marshall, 1842-1924," *The Economic Journal*, 34 (135): 311–72.

_____ (1936), *The General Theory of Employment, Interest and Money,* New York: Harcourt Brace Jovanovich.

Keynes, J.N. (1891), republished 1955 in *The Scope and Method of Political Economy*, 4th ed., New York: Kelley and Millman, Inc. (London: Macmillan.)

Klamer, Arjo (1984), *Conversations with Economists,* Totowa, NJ: Rowman and Allanheld.

_____ and D. Colander (1990), *The Making of an Economist,* Boulder, CO: Westview Press.

Klein, L. *et al.* (1991), "Lessons from Half a Century of Macroeconomic Modeling," in R.G. Bodkin, L.R. Klein and K. Marwah, A *History of Macroeconomic Model Building,* Aldershot, UK: Edward Elgar.

Kreps, D. (1997), "Economics—The Current Position," *Daedalus*, Winter.

Krueger, A. *et al.* (1991), *Journal of Economic Literature,* September: 1035–53.

Kydland, F. and E. Prescott (1977) "Rules Rather than Discretion: The Inconsistency of Optimal Plans," *Journal of Political Economy*, (June): 473–91.

Leamer, E. (1978), *Specification Searches: Ad Hoc Inferences with Nonexperimental Data,* New York: John Wiley.

_____ (1983), "Let's Take the Con out of Econometrics," *American Economic Review*, 73 (March): 31–43.

Leimer, D. and D.L. Selig(1982), "Social Security and Private Saving: New Time-series Evidence," *Journal of Political Economy,* 90 (3) (June): 606–29.

Lucas, R. (1984), in A. Klamer, *Conversations with Economists,* Totowa, NJ: Rowman and Allanheld.

Machlup, F. (1963), *Essays on Economics Semantics*, Englewood Cliffs, NJ: Prentice Hall.

Maddison, A. (1995), *Monitoring the World Economy, 1820–1992*, Washington, DC: Organization for Economic Cooperation and Development.

_____ (1999), "Poor Until 1920," *The Wall Street Journal*, 1 January.

Mankiw, N.G. (1998), *Economics,* San Diego, CA: Dryden Press.

Marshall, A. (1902), "A Plea for the Creation of a Curriculum in Economics and Associated Branches of Political Science," reprinted in A. Marshall (1961), *Principles of Economics,* vol. 2, annotated by C.W. Guillebaud), pp. 161–77, London: Macmillan and Company Limited.

_____ (1961), *Principles of Economics,* vols. 1 and 2, 9th edition, annotated by C.W. Guillebaud, London: Macmillan and Company Limited.

Marx, K. (1847), *The Misery of Philosophy.*

Mayer T. (1993a), *Truth versus Precision in Economics*, Aldershot, UK: Edward Elgar.

_____ (1993b), "Friedman's Methodology of Positive Economics: a Soft Reading," *Economic Inquiry* (April).

_____ (1997), "Data Mining: A Reconsideration," Davis, CA: University of California at Davis, Davis Working Paper 97–15, April.

McCloskey, D.N. (1985), *The Rhetoric of Economics*, Madison: University of Wisconsin Press.

_____ and Ziliak, S.T. (1996), "The Standard Error of Regressions," *Journal of Economic Literature*, March.

McConnell, C.R. and S.L. Brue (1990), *Economics: Principles, Problems, and Policies,* New York: McGraw-Hill Publishing Co.

_____ and S. Brue (1999), *Economics*, Burr Ridge, IL: McGraw Hill.

Mitchell, W.C. (1967), *Types of Economic Theory*, 2 vols., ed. Joseph Dorfman, New York: Kelley.

Niehans, J. (1990), *A History of Economic Theory: Classic Contributions, 1720–1980,* Baltimore and London: The Johns Hopkins University Press.

North, D. and R.P. Thomas (1973), *The Rise of the Western World*, Cambridge, UK: Cambridge University Press.

Peirce, C. (1960), "Notes on Scientific Philosophy" in Charles Hartshorne and Paul Weiss (eds), *Collected Papers of Charles Sanders Peirce*, vol. 1, pp. 50–72, Cambridge: Harvard University Press.

Quirmbach, H.C. (1993), 'R&D: Competition, Risk, and Performance," *Rand Journal of Economics*, 24 (Summer).

Roll, E. (1938, 1942), *A History of Economic Thought*, London; New York: Faber and Faber; Prentice-Hall.

Rosenberg, A. (1992), *Economics—Mathematical Politics or Science of Diminishing Returns,* Chicago: University of Chicago Press.

Rosenberg, N. (1994), *Exploring the Black Box: Technology, Economics, and History,* Cambridge, England, and New York: Cambridge University Press.

_____ and L.E. Birdzell Jr. (1986), *How the West Grew Rich: The Economic Transformation of the Industrial World,* New York: Basic Books.

Roughgarden, J. (1996), *Primer of Ecological Theory,* Upper Saddle River, NJ: Prentice Hall.

Samuelson, P. (1947), *Foundations of Economic Analysis,* Cambridge: Harvard University Press.

_____ (1955), *Economics: An Introductory Analysis*, 3rd ed., New York: McGraw-Hill.

_____ and W.D. Nordhaus (1989), *Economics*, 13th ed., New York: McGraw Hill Book Company

Say, J.B. (1848), *Treastise on Political Economy,* 6th ed.

Schumpeter, J.A. (1954), *History of Economic Analysis*, ed. E. B. Schumpeter, London: George Allen and Unwin.

Screpanti, E. and S. Zamagni (1993), *An Outline of the History of Economic Thought*, Oxford: Clarendon Press.

Solow, R. (1994), "Review of Thomas Mayer's *Truth and Precision in Economics,*" *Journal of Economic Methodology*.

_____ (1997), "How Did Economics Get that Way and What Way Did it Get?" *Daedalus,* (Winter): 39–58.

Spiegel, H.W. (1991), *The Growth of Economic Thought*, 3rd ed., London: Duke University Press.

Stigler, G.J. (1941), *Production and Distribution Theories*, New York: Macmillan.

Szenberg, M. (1998), *Passion and Craft*, Ann Arbor: University of Michigan Press.

Veblen, T. (1900), "Preconceptions of Economic Science," *Quarterly Journal of Economics*, 14 (February): 261.

Viner, J. (1931), "Cost Curves and Supply Curves," *Zeitschrift für Nationaloekonomie,*" reprinted in *Readings in Price Theory*, American Economic Association, Homewood, IL: Irwin, 1952.

Von Neumann, J. (1928), "Zur Theorie Der Gesellschaftsspiele," *Mathematische Annalen,* 100: 295–320.

_____ and O. Morgenstern (1944), *Theory of Games and Economic Behavior*, Princeton: Princeton University Press.

Weiner, S.E. (1993), "New Estimates of the Natural Rate of Unemployment," *Federal Reserve Bank of Kansas City Economic Review*, 4th Quarter, 53–69.

_____ (1994), "The Natural Rate and Inflationary Pressures," *Federal Reserve Bank of Kansas City Economic Review*, 3rd Quarter, 5–9.

_____ (1995), "Challenges to the Natural Rate Framework," *Federal Reserve Bank of Kansas City Economic Review*, 2nd Quarter, 19–25.

Woodward, M. (1991), "Self-fulfilling Expectations and Fluctuations in Aggregate Demand" in G. Mankiw and D. Romer, *New Keynesian Economics*, Cambridge, MA: MIT Press.

Yang, X. and S. Ng (1994), "Specialization and Division of Labor: A Survey," *Seminar Paper* 24/95, Department of Economics, Monash University, December.

Index